CITY GIRL – THE EARLY YEARS (2011-2015)

CITY GIRL – THE EARLY YEARS (2011-2015)

LINDA BRENDLE

Linda Brendle

Copyright © 2023 by Linda Brendle

All rights reserved. No part of this book may be reproduced in any manner whatsoever without written permission except in the case of brief quotations embodied in critical articles and reviews.

First Printing, 2023

CONTENTS

DEDICATION		**1**
1	Memories of Earl Hill – 4/02/19	2
IN THE BEGINNING		**5**
2	Your Tax Dollars at Work – 9/7/11	6
3	Victims of the Texas Drought – 2/20/12	9
4	Presentation Isn't Everything – 4/28/12	11
5	When Did This Become My Job? – 5/2/12	14
COUNTRY GIRL STUFF		**19**
6	Puppies, Wasps, & Every Day Heroes – 7/18/12	20
7	I'm a City Girl and I Hate Bugs – 5/3/13	24
8	I Love Trees – Sometimes – 7/6/14	27
9	Country Girls Have Septic Tanks – 3/7/15	29
10	Lessons from the Storm – 4/26/15	31
11	In Danger of Losing My Identity – 5/23/15	34
12	Can you cut up a chicken? – 9/7/15	37

GARDENING — 41

13   I Planted a Scraggly Garden – 5/27/12   42

14   Return on Investment - Plant the Seeds and Watch the Increase – 10/7/12   46

15   Success Is a Two-Inch Tomato! – 11/29/12   49

16   Plans, God, and Day Lilies – 3/24/13   52

17   From Trash to Watermelons – 4/13/13   55

18   Garlic Wars Escalate in Emory – 5/7/13   58

19   Preemptive Harvest Ends Garlic Wars – 5/23/13   60

20   Am I Smarter Than a Fifth Grader? – 6/18/13   62

21   What I Did This Summer – 9/06/13   65

22   Attention North Texas Gardeners - It's Time to Plant Onions – 1/28/14   68

23   Odd Beginnings Can Yield Beautiful Fruit – 2/26/14   70

24   Stewardship and Planting Trees – 4/27/14   73

25   That Garden Will Preach – 5/31/14   76

26   Four More Lessons from My Garden – 7/13/14   79

27   Texas Dirt – 8/03/14   82

28   Faith, Garlic, and Gophers – 10/19/14   85

29   Gardeners Learn to Adjust – 3/22/15   87

FAITH — 91

30   The Party's not Over – 1/16/13   92

31	Christmas Came Early This Year – 12/19/13	96
32	Scavenger Hunt – 21st Century Style – 3/28/14	99
33	The Surprises & Promises of Spring – 4/05/14	102
34	Church Ladies – 5/24/14	104
35	Church Ladies: from the Other Side – 8/25/14	107
36	Wishing You a Messy Christmas – 12/14/14	110
37	The Promise Never Changes – 12/21/14	113
38	Post-Christmas Decisions – 1/03/15	116
39	Valentine's Day - Not Just a Hallmark Holiday – 2/14/14	118
40	Granddaughters, Broken Hearts, and Good Friday – 3/29/15	121
41	Fat and Happy – 8/2/15	124
42	The Church Kitchen – 8/9/15	126
43	Advent is a Season of Hope – 11/29/15	129
44	Advent is a Season of Peace – 12/6/15	132
45	Advent is a Season of Joy – 12/13/15	135
46	Advent is a Season of Love – 12/20/15	137

FAMILY AND FRIENDS — **141**

47	The Nature of Generosity – 6/12/12	142
48	Quality Family Time – 7/26/12	145
49	The Schutters, Moving on Up – 5/21/13	149

50	Haute Cuisine or Country Cookin' – 5/2/14	152
51	On Motherhood, Co-Dependence, and Letting Go – 5/10/14	154
52	Family, Football, and Chili Cook-Offs – 10/27/14	157
53	Is There Birthday Cake In Heaven? – 11/2/14	159
54	The Part of the Story the Veterans Don't Tell – 11/9/14	161
55	Music and Alzheimer's: The Memories of Music Live On – 2/22/15	164
56	A Very Special Graduate – and Grandpa's Nerd – 6/3/15	167
57	The Truck Stop Crawl – 8/16/15	170
58	A Common Bond of Brothers – 10/11/15	172

WARNING SIGNS OF ALZHEIMER'S — **175**

59	Part 1 of 10 – Memory Changes that Disrupt Daily Life – 10/17/13	176
60	Part 2 of 10 – Challenges in Planning or Solving Problems – 10/24/13	179
61	Part 3 of 10 – Difficulty Completing Familiar Tasks at Home, at Work or at Leisure – 11/3/13	182
62	Part 4 of 10 – Confusion with Time and Place – 11/9/13	185
63	Part 5 of 10 - Trouble Understanding Visual Images and Spatial Relationships – 11/13/13	188

64	Part 6 of 10 – New Difficulties with Words when Speaking or Writing – 11/30/13	191
65	Part 7 of 10 – Misplacing Things and Losing the Ability to Retrace Steps – 12/5/13	194
66	Part 8 of 10 – Changes in Judgment – 12/11/13	197
67	Part 9 of 10 - Withdrawal from Work or Social Activities – 1/05/14	199
68	Part 10 of 10 - Changes in Mood and Personality – 1/28/14	202

COMMUNITY — 205

69	Veterans Are Treated with Dignity in Emory, Texas – 11/13/13	206
70	Thanksgiving in April – 4/13/14	209
71	Democracy in Emory – 3/14/15	211
72	Community – 7/5/15	213
73	Observations from the County Fair – 9/20/15	216

THE WHEAT BELLY DIET — 219

74	The Great Brendle Wheat Belly Experiment – 3/7/14	220
75	Wheat Belly Update: Baby Steps – 3/15/14	223
76	Wheat Belly Update: The Next Step – 3/23/14	225

HUMOR — 227

77	Final Solutions - Graveyard Humor - 8/13/14	228
78	When I Don't Have a Schedule – 11/30/14	230

79	Four Christmas Gift Fails – 12/7/14	233
80	The Downsizing of America – 1/13/15	236
81	Ten Things That Can Make You Feel Old (and what to do about them) – 1/25/15	238
82	Bugs – Betcha Can't Eat Just One – 4/05/15	241
83	Is It "Smartphone Face or Just a Double Chin? – 4/14/15	243
84	Ten Ways to Know You're Getting Older – 4/19/15	245
85	The Silliness of Soap – 5/17/15	247
86	Senior Humor – 10/19/15	250
87	More Senior Humor – 10/25/15	253
88	There's a National Month for Everything – 11/1/15	256

WRITING — 259

89	Anaiah Press Accepted My Memoir: Will Publication Make a Difference – 1/19/14	260
90	The Glamour of Being an Author – 5/19/14	262
91	Waiting Room Characters and Stories – 6/14/14	264
92	Tributes to Those We Love – 6/29/14	267
93	Five Ways to Write a Memoir without Being Disowned – 8/17/14	270
94	On Being a Celebrity – 2/8/15	274
95	Hiding In the Luggage – 3/1/15	276

CONTENTS - XI

LOOKING BACK — **279**

96	Beatlemania Affected Even Small Town Texas – 2/08/14	280
97	Healthcare - Then and Now – 7/27/14	283
98	For Mattias: How TV Was Different when I Was a Kid – 8/31/14	286
99	How TV Programming Was Different when I Was a Kid – 9/7/14	288
100	We Dressed Differently when I Was a Kid – 9/14/14	291
101	The Value of a Penny Was a Lot Different When I Was a Kid – 9/28/14	294
102	Cars Were a Lot Different When I Was a Kid – 10/5/14	297
103	Grandparents Were a Lot Different when I Was a Kid – 10/12/14	299
104	A Walk Down Memory Lane – 21st Century Style – 6/7/15	302
105	How did we survive? – 7/19/15	304

POTPOURRI — **307**

106	Feeling Old – 1/18/15	308
107	It's the Small Things – 2/01/15	310
108	Nightwalk for Hope Rained Out – 5/10/15	313
109	Mass Shooters: Are they shouting, "Look at me?" – 6/30/15	316

110	The ladies of the Order of the Pink Ribbon – 11/8/15	319
111	Getting off the Interstate – 11/15/15	322
112	New Year's Day - What's It All About? – 12/27/14	325

ABOUT THE AUTHOR   329

MORE BOOKS BY LINDA BRENDLE   331

DEDICATION

To Earl Hill who printed my first submissions and gave me the byline *City Girl*; and to Trey Hill who has kept the family tradition alive at the **Rains County Leader.**

CHAPTER 1

Memories of Earl Hill – 4/02/19

A spray of white roses adorning the door of the *Rains County Leader* is a testament to the love and respect given to a life well lived. Earl C. Hill, Jr., owner, publisher, and former editor of the *Leader* died on March 27, and he will be missed. I don't have a lot of personal memories of Mr. Hill, but the few I have are good ones.

David and I moved to Emory in February, 2011, and I submitted my first article to the *Leader* in September of that year. The titled of it was "Your Tax Dollars at Work," and it was about the Senior Center. Participation in the weekday lunch program was down, and there was concern that the program would be dropped. My purpose in writing the article was to introduce the service to anyone who might not know about it and to encourage seniors to try it out for the first time or to come back. I didn't hear back from Mr. Hill, so I assumed he didn't like what I had to say – but then my article appeared in the paper in the "Letters to the Editor" section.

I wrote another article or two over the next several months, and each one was printed. Then, in January of 2012, I received a phone call from Mr. Hill. He said that he had checked out my blog, and that he liked what I wrote. He also said that any time I wanted to submit something, he would print it. I'm sure there were limits to that offer, but I guess I never pushed them too far. True to his word, he printed everything I submitted – with the exception of one column in which I mentioned that we were out of town. Company policy didn't allow articles that might notify thieves of a potential target. He even gave me a column with a byline at the beginning and a brief bio at the end.

At first, I wrote when the spirit moved me, but I began to develop a small following at the Senior Center. People began asking me on Monday or Tuesday if I had a column in that week's paper, and some were disappointed if I said no. Some even based their decision of whether to buy a paper on my answer, so I began to feel an obligation, both to my readers and to the paper, to become more regular in my writing. The final push to weekly submissions came when Mr. Hill gave my column a title.

Mom and Dad were both raised on farms in West Texas, but they had long since moved to the city by the time I was born. Until David and I bought our two-plus acres in Rains County, I had never coped up close and personal with the realities of country living. A lot of my columns dealt with the struggles of adjusting – and then I decided to plant a garden. Oh, the writing material! There was wind, rain, drought, bugs, leaf mold and fungus, garlic-eating gophers, tomato-eating squirrels, leaf-eating deer, and much more. I moaned and complained that people from the city didn't know how to deal with such things, and one Tuesday morning, I discovered that I had become "City Girl."

All my correspondence with the Leader is done electronically, and I only remember meeting Mr. Hill face to face one time. I believe it was the winter of 2012 when David and I stopped by the Leader office for the Christmas Open House. We met several staff members, and then one of them introduced us to the owner himself. He took us on a personal tour of the building, showing us pictures of earlier offices and owners and explaining the inner workings of the operation. It was obvious that he was proud of the results of his life's work, and with good reason.

I didn't know Earl Hill, but based on the care with which he oversaw the operation of the *Leader,* it was obvious that he was a man of conviction and principle. He knew what kind of paper he wanted to produce, and he refused to bow to money-making trends or gimmicks if it meant violating his principles. On the other hand, he didn't hesitate to take a chance on something he liked, even if it was a writer like me who had no experience or references to offer. Thank you, Mr. Hill, and may God continue to bless the legacy and memories you left behind.

IN THE BEGINNING

CHAPTER 2

Your Tax Dollars at Work – 9/7/11

David and I went to the Senior Center for lunch today. Several people waved at us as we signed in. I headed toward the take-one-leave-one bookshelf with the paperback David finished last night. It took me a little while to get there.

"Hey, how're you doing today?"

"Good to see you."

"I saved you and David a seat."

I smiled, returned greetings, and deposited my book. I didn't take one. I still owe one more before I'm even. I got back to the steam table as David got his plate. Enchiladas, rice, and green beans today. Looked good.

We go to the Senior Center for lunch almost every day. We learned about it from one of our neighbors when we moved here in February. She begged us to come. The number of participants was low, sometimes only thirty or forty a day, and the caterer was threatening to pull out of the program.

The Senior Meal Program is a Title III program that falls under "Special Programs for the Aging." It's one of those "entitlement" programs that conservatives like me sometimes object to, at least in principal. I was a little embarrassed at first to take a free lunch, literally and figuratively. But at the time, we were dry camping in our RV while we repaired the damage inflicted on our mobile home by the latest renters. After spending the morning pulling up carpet ruined by animals, painting sub-flooring with Kilz, or scrubbing walls yellowed by nicotine, it was such a relief to run down to the Center for lunch that I didn't object much. The paperwork we filled out emphasized that the program was available to anyone over 60, regardless of income or other need criteria. My aunt, whose counsel I value highly, told me that we seniors need to take advantage of every benefit offered to us, and there's a donation box available for voluntary contributions. The deciding factor was that David loved going to the Center, so I swallowed my pride, and we became regulars.

It's now six months later, and we've been living in the mobile home for a while. We have kitchen appliances, new carpeting and tile, fresh paint, and only a faint lingering odor of dog mixed with cigarette smoke. We have the time and the energy to fix lunch at home, but we still go to the Center most days. Due to some publicity in the Rains County Leader and lots of word-of-mouth advertising, we now have at least seventy people a day and sometimes as many as 100, not counting the thirty or so homebound recipients. The food is good, but the company is better. Over the months, we've made some really good friends, and we've seen the faces and heard the stories behind the program.

One lady is a widow with a bright smile and a fanatical interest in the Texas Rangers. After her husband died and before she started coming to the center, she sat at home alone, waiting to die. One ex-Navy man has lots of stories, and on Memorial Day he prepared and presented a program for his fellow seniors. There are couples and singles, blacks and whites, snappy dressers and Goodwill rejects, those who drive nice cars and those who depend on the program's bus or a ride from a friend. Some depend on the lunch they eat at the Center and the meal they take home for dinner as their main source of nutrition. Many depend on the social interaction to relieve an otherwise solitary life.

We're all a family, and we watch out for each other. We smile and hug, we play Mexican Train or 42, we work on jigsaw puzzles, we eat, we chat. The Center manager hovers over all of us, making sure we get enough to eat, even those of us who are picky eaters. When my neighbor isn't feeling well, I get a meal to go for her. When her car isn't working, we take turns picking her up. When someone needs a ride to the beauty shop or the doctor or the grocery store, there's always someone to provide it. And if you need a wagon…

"I have a fig tree I'm trying to save" said one lady. "It's a long way from the house, so I have to tote water out there."

"You need a wagon," I said.

"Oh, I have one," offered someone.

"I guess we need to get you one," suggested someone else.

"Could you use a wheel barrow?" said another gentleman.

"That would work."

"You got it. I've got two. I'll bring one tomorrow."

And he did.

So what have I learned? I've learned the real meaning of the idiom "walk a mile in my shoes." I've learned to check out the faces and the stories behind the entitlement. I've learned that government programs sometimes hand out a lot more than a free lunch.

CHAPTER 3

Victims of the Texas Drought – 2/20/12

One of the things that attracted us to the two-plus acres we now call home was the abundance of trees. Out of curiosity, David once took an inventory and counted eighty-five. Now we have two less.

We had two large red oaks behind the northeast corner of the house, one with a double trunk and the other with one trunk. They were about seventy-five feet tall and were around seventy-five years old. They weren't located in the most convenient spot. We have a fifty-amp outlet on that corner of the house, and that's where we park the motor home. But David's pretty good at wrangling that forty-foot monster around, so he backed it in between the house and the double-trunked oak and nosed it in between the two trees. The oaks seemed to be a favorite with the birds and the squirrels, and they gave great shade to the house, the shed, and all the vehicles. And then the drought came.

We watered some, but we don't have a well, and city water is expensive and restricted. About mid-summer the leaves started to turn brown, and we hoped they were just going into hibernation to conserve moisture. But the leaves didn't fall, so we feared the worst. We wanted to wait until Spring to see if they recovered, but then the bark started to peel off in sheets. The trunks were soon covered with a dry, dusty green fungus, but we still waited. Then the Texas winds started to blow, and the limbs started to drop. At first it was just small branches that landed mostly in the driveway. Then they got a little bigger, and one poked a hole in one of the RV awnings. Finally, when we found a couple of widow-making limbs standing straight up with several inches buried in the ground, we knew it was time to act.

We have some pretty versatile neighbors. One of them is an expert tree surgeon, and his prices are right, so we enlisted his help. He didn't use any fancy tools or lifts, just a ladder, some ropes, a pole saw, and a chain saw, but he knew what he was doing. He was careful to cut the limbs in front of his perch instead of behind, and if a limb threatened to fall on the house or the shed, he tied it off and lowered it with a rope. When one of the limbs knocked over his ladder, I was concerned, but he rappelled down the trunk of the tree like it was no big deal.

We had one casualty. Our rail fence took a direct hit, but it was left by the renters, so it's no big loss. And we ended up with a mess. It's a shame we don't have a fireplace, but the neighbors - some of whom came by to watch the show - will help with that. Several have offered to help clean up and haul off in exchange for some firewood.

So now we have eighty-three trees. We'll have a lot less shade on the house, but once we get the stumps burned out, it will be easier to park the RV. We've lost several other trees, too, but their falling limbs are not endangering anything, so we'll wait a while longer to take them down. For now, we'll say good-bye to two beautiful trees and continue to pray for an end to the drought.

CHAPTER 4

Presentation Isn't Everything – 4/28/12

I don't know if it's Emory in particular or small towns in general, but there are a lot of potlucks around here. In the fourteen months since I've been here I've taken food to several lunches for bereaved families, desserts to the Senior Center on Volunteer Dessert Day several times, muffins and juice to a church-wide breakfast, soup to a SISTAs luncheon, cookies to AWANA, a salad to one baptism/potluck and a dessert to another, and those are just the ones I can remember right now. This morning I baked cookies for a Sunday School party tonight and made a cake for a spaghetti lunch after church tomorrow. The SISTAs ministry is raising funds for a youth mission trip to China.

I like to cook, and I'm pretty good at it, but when you take food to an "event," there's some expectation that it look good as well as taste good. Let's just say I was absent the day they taught presentation in Home Ec or was standing behind the door when the Martha Stewart genes were passed out. I think my friend Mary got my share. She can make a simple snack of cheese, crackers, and fruit look like a feast, and her baked goods always look like they came fresh from the most elegant bakery in town. She says the secret is paper doilies on the platter, but I can never find paper doilies in the store - and the rare occasions when I have them, I never have the right size.

My lack of presentation skills isn't a problem at home because I serve the plates in the kitchen, and David doesn't care what it looks like once it gets to the table as long as he has a fork or spoon handy. It's not even much of a problem when we have company. I have a few nice serving bowls and platters, and I usually serve buffet style. Once the first person is through the line, the presentation is lost anyway. But I always feel inadequate when it comes to taking food somewhere.

First of all, I don't have any of the cute carry-along containers that every other woman who ever attends a potluck seems to have. When I take a hot casserole, instead of a baking dish with its own lid, cozy insulated zippered case, and convenient carrying handles, I end up covering my dish with aluminum foil, putting it on a cookie sheet or in a cardboard box, and surrounding it with towels in the hopes that it will be at least slightly above room temperature at serving time.

I try to avoid taking cakes, because mine have a tendency to cling to the pan with great tenacity. When I get brave and lucky enough to end up with a whole cake, I don't have one of those cute tole-painted cake carriers with hinged clasps to secure the top to the base. Instead, I have a monstrous Tupperware antique that no longer snaps and burps and whose handles have long since gone the way of all small plastic items that you knew were in that drawer just last week. On the other hand, if I decide to take a pre-sliced cake or cookies, my serving trays are never the right size or shape, and my careful arrangements always look haphazard by the time I arrive at my destination.

The funny thing is, nobody seems to notice the odd appearance of my offerings except me. Maybe they notice but are too polite to mention it, or maybe they look beyond the appearance and see the spirit with which it's offered. At any rate, by the end of the evening my dishes seem to be as empty as all the others, and no one goes away hungry.

It's about time to finish this up and get ready for the party tonight. I'm looking forward to some fun and fellowship and to some really good food. My cookies got a little too brown on the bottom, but David ate two at lunch and didn't complain, so I guess they'll do. I'm looking forward to tomorrow's lunch, too. My cake stuck again, so I guess I'll slice it up. I'm also supposed to take a loaf of French bread, so when I go to the store to pick it up, I'll see if I can find one of those disposable aluminum platters for the cake. I wonder if they have paper doilies.

CHAPTER 5

When Did This Become My Job? – 5/2/12

I joined a work party last week to paint the inside of the Senior Center here in Emory. It's an older building that has been well used and was in need of a face lift. The director secured a small grant for carpet for the entry hall and offices, paint, tile for a backsplash in the kitchen, blinds, and three baseboard heaters, but she didn't have enough money left to cover labor costs. Our church, Believers' Baptist, is always on the lookout for "Outside the Building" projects, so David and I stopped by the pastor's office on the way home from lunch one day to discuss the possibilities. A couple of phone calls and a visit or two later, David was asked to head up the project and a call for volunteers went out.

As we pulled into the parking lot Friday morning, we were a little nervous. The Center can only be closed a certain number of days a year, and considering all the holidays already scheduled, closing it Friday and Monday was pushing the limit. The carpet was scheduled to go in Monday, so it was critical that we get the painting done in a couple of days. The Center isn't huge, but it would be a huge job for two people. What if no one else showed up?

We shouldn't have worried. We arrived at the appointed time, but several people were there ahead of us. A Center employee had an urn of coffee made and a cooler of ice water ready. A couple from the church was rolling out brown paper to protect the tile floors and putting masking tape around the baseboards while one of the Center's clients removed nails and screws from the walls. Others drifted in, looked around for a job, and started to work. One gentleman who was not feeling well enough to work made a run to the donut shop so we'd have something to go with our coffee.

I hate prep work, and my hands aren't steady enough for trim work, so I rolled. I'm pretty good with a roller, but I'm also pretty messy. I got almost as much paint on the walls as I did on myself, but I've come to expect that. I have a pair of jeans and a t-shirt that make up my designated painting outfit. Both are decorated with the colors of the inside and outside of our home, a little of the color of the school doors we helped paint last summer, and now the new Senior Center color as well. In addition to being messy, I'm also short, so I painted the low sections of the walls while those less height challenged painted the higher sections. Luckily they were not as messy as I am, so I didn't end up with paint in my hair, but I did end up with sore legs from all the squatting.

We had a total of eleven volunteers. We worked well together and moved seamlessly from one room to the other, from one task to the next. Before anyone had time to get too tired or cranky, the painting was done and clean-up was in progress. David thanked everyone profusely for their help, and we were home in time for a late lunch.

Looking back on the experience, I wondered what motivates people to volunteer for a difficult, messy job like painting the Senior Center. Some of us, like David and me and the man who was taking down the screws and nails, have a vested interest. We eat and socialize there, and it will be a more pleasant experience now. But most of the workers had never been inside the Center, and several won't be eligible for its services for another decade or two. All of them gave up several hours of their time, and some even took off work. Why would they choose to pick up a paint brush; what was in it for them? Is it the simple satisfaction of a job well done, or is there more to it than that?

As a society, we seem to have developed a strong sense of division of labor in a lot of areas of our lives. At work we're very conscious of what we're being paid to do and what is above or below our pay grade. At home, children and adults alike argue over whose job it is to take out the trash or do the dishes, and the media loves stories about the constant battle of responsibilities between government, school, church, and family. So what makes a person choose to do something for which they receive no measurable benefit?

When I was growing up, that question would be answered by quoting scripture: "Do to others as you would like them to do to you," and "When you did it to one of the least of these my brothers and sisters, you were doing it to me." Quoting the Bible is not as politically correct as it once was, so now you hear phrases like "random acts of kindness," "paying it forward," and "doing the right thing." There is plenty of material that tells us we should be helpful and charitable, but I don't have a clue what moves us to take that step forward and say "I'll do it."

There's another verse in Ecclesiastes that says something like "Whatever your hand find to do, do it with your might." I've always taken that verse to mean, when you have a job to do, do it well. I still think that's a valid interpretation, but what struck me this morning was the first word, whatever. What that says to me is when you see a job that needs doing, whatever it is, whether it's your job or not, do it and do it well. Maybe that's what sparked those volunteers at the Senior Center and all the others who are paying it forward or helping the least of these. They saw a job that needed doing and decided it was their job.

COUNTRY GIRL STUFF

CHAPTER 6

Puppies, Wasps, & Every Day Heroes – 7/18/12

Last Monday was an eventful day in a country living kind of way. It started normally enough with breakfast followed by coffee in front of our respective laptops, checking to see what was going on in the rest of the world. Neither of us found anything particularly interesting, so David put on his work boots and hat and went out to do battle with another tree stump, and I went to the garden to pull weeds. He told me later that when he was getting his tools, he heard a low growl under the shed. I would have investigated immediately, but his focus on the task at hand was stronger than his curiosity, so I was the first to meet our visitor. As I knelt in the garden, a little furball barreled into my backside.

"Well, who are you?" I said.

The little black and white puppy rolled over and showed me his tummy. He didn't have a collar, and he wasn't talking, so I went back to weeding. He tried to help, but he had trouble distinguishing between the weeds and the tomato plants, so I evicted him from the garden. He didn't stay evicted long, so I took him over and introduced him to David. He wasn't much help with the tree stump either, so we went back to the garden where I tried not to step on him, trip over him, or stab him with a weeding tool.

I also tried to ignore him, hoping he'd get bored and go home. He was so little, probably not much more than a month old, and it was unlikely he could find his way home, even if home was close enough for his little legs to make the trip. It was more likely that some irresponsible pet owner had found a sparsely populated area away from traffic and dumped him. He was a friendly little thing and too cute for words, but I knew we couldn't keep him. We don't have a fence, and the open floor plan of our house doesn't offer anywhere to pen up a rambunctious puppy. A third family member makes travel more complicated, and another mouth to feed adds another expense. I tried not to think about how long it had been since he had eaten.

When I went in to clean up for lunch, he followed me up the stairs, whining and scratching at the door when I closed it, leaving him outside. David came in soon afterward, and we didn't talk much about the elephant in the room or the puppy on the porch. We hoped someone at the Senior Center would know where he came from or would want to take him in.

"Do you want a puppy?" we said to several of our neighbors.

"No," was the almost unanimous response; however, Mary who lives around the curve from us made an offer.

"I can't keep him," she said, "but I'll take him and see if I can find where he came from. If I can't, I'll put him on Craig's list and find him a home."

When we got home, we didn't see him, but we heard a rustle under the front porch. A little black nose appeared by the bottom step, and he wriggled his fat little body through the gap between the steps and the skirting.

"He's probably thirsty. It's getting pretty warm out here," said David.

Now that The Mutt as David called him had somewhere to go, it seemed okay to offer him a little hospitality that might otherwise have given him the wrong idea about our intentions. I brought him some water, but he wasn't impressed, so I brought him a little milk. He buried his nose in the bowl and didn't take a breath until he'd licked it clean.

"Want some more?" I said.

He did, and he finished it with equal enthusiasm. After his third round, he let out a satisfied burp, curled up in a ball, and went to sleep. I went inside to do some laundry, but when it clouded up and cooled off a bit, I went outside to visit with The Mutt before Mary came to pick him up. I got a bucket and policed the area for the bits of trash that seem to surface every time it rains. He helped, biting at the pieces of glass I unearthed and chasing my toes when I moved from place to place.

In a few minutes, Mary pulled into the driveway and smiled as I picked him up and walked over to her window.

"You're a real cutie, aren't you?" she said, taking him gently from me and cradling him comfortably against her shoulder. I was a little sad as she drove away, but I knew it was best for him. She was rescuing him from becoming one of the homeless dogs that wanders the back roads around here or something worse. Some of the long-time country folks at the Senior Center assured me that if someone didn't take him in, he'd be on a coyote's dinner table by morning.

Before he was out of sight, it began to sprinkle a bit, so I decided to call it a day. I went to empty my bucket, but when I got to the trash barrel, it was raining so hard I forgot to watch for the red wasps that hang around that end of the house. By the time I remembered, it was too late. As I turned my bucket up over the barrel, I felt a stabbing pain in my wrist. I dropped my bucket, slapped at my wrist, and vacated the area ASAP. I almost collided with David who was headed for the house, too.

"A wasp got me," I said, showing him my wrist that was already beginning to swell a bit.

I applied a couple of the anti-bite and anti-itch remedies we've collected and didn't think much more about it. We both turned on our computers and did some surfing until the shower passed and the sun came back out. Then David disappeared into the laundry room and came out with three cans of insect spray of various kinds and went outside. In a few minutes he opened the door and stuck his head in.

"That roach spray works real well on wasps. Come and see."

I followed him out and looked where he pointed. There were a dozen or so wasps on the ground, suffering the fatal effects of David's wrath.

"I may not have gotten the one that got you, but I got a bunch of them."

That was our country living day: a puppy, a wasp, and a couple of heroes. I'm not sure why God made wasps. I know bees pollinate fruit and flowers, but what good are wasps? It's a little easier to understand why He made dogs. Some of them are useful, and those who aren't are cuddly and good company. But I'm pretty sure why He made heroes. There are times when you're down on your luck and don't have anywhere to go, or when you've been hurt by the stinging things of life, and you need somebody to step up and say *I can help*. That's why God made people like Mary and David, friends and loved ones who can be our every day heroes when we need them.

CHAPTER 7

I'm a City Girl and I Hate Bugs – 5/3/13

One of the bad things about living in the country is the bugs. I've come a long way in the two years we lived here. I no longer scream and flail around when a multi-legged creature lands on me – at least not much. I've even been known to pick a lady bug or other benign insect off a leaf and evict it from my garden with my bare hands. But there are limits to my tolerance, and those limits were reached several times this week.

This is the time of year when the weather is conducive to open windows. I love feeling the cool breeze blowing through, replacing the stale winter air with the fresh smells of spring, but there are negative aspects, too. There's dust and there are bugs. Our screens are getting old. They don't fit as tightly as they used to, and if there's the least little open space, all kinds of creepy-crawlies and flying things find their way in. I've gotten used to it, and many a bug has found himself in the bowels of the vacuum cleaner bag before he knew what hit him.

I'm not so calm when it comes to spiders, though, and this week there was a spider. A big one. In the bathtub. We don't use the tub much. It's a big round thing that looks impressive but isn't really. It's fairly shallow and doesn't have any jets, and we can empty our 40-gallon hot water tank without filling it up enough for a really good soak. Even so, I wasn't thrilled when a big black eight-legged thing took up residence in it. I didn't think he could crawl up the slick fiberglass sides, but you never know what they can do with those webs, so I kept a wary eye on him. Several times I thought he was dead, but then he'd make another circuit around the tub, plotting his escape and the evil he'd inflict on me once he got out. Finally, enough was enough, and I got out the bug spray. After a squirt or two, I left him to his fate, and after he was sufficiently shriveled to pose no threat, I picked him up with a tissue and sent him to a watery grave in the septic tank.

Things were quiet in the bug wars for a day or two, but they heated up on Wednesday night when I was fixing dinner. I had been out to the garden for some lettuce and was rinsing away the sand when I felt a tickle on the back of my knee. I didn't think much about it. I had on jeans, so what could it be? Maybe a drop of sweat although it wasn't really that hot. Then I felt it again, more of a scratching sensation this time. I reached down and felt a lump under the denim. I don't know if the Guinness Book of World Records has an entry for this category, but I'm pretty sure I broke the speed record for getting out of a pair of jeans. It was only a cricket, but he paid dearly for his invasion of my privacy. He ended his days wadded up in a paper towel in the trash can. It might have been a bug's idea of Heaven except there are no food scraps there. They're all on the compost pile where all the smart bugs go for dinner.

You'd think that was enough excitement for one day, but the close encounters continued. That night when I went to the bathroom to get ready for bed I heard a flying creature of some sort banging himself again and again against the mirrors and light fixtures. I ignored him while I went through my nightly routine. The final ritual is the taking of the pills. While I was getting a large white caplet from one bottle and a medium-sized pink one from another, I realized I didn't hear the bug any more. I looked around on the counter but didn't see him, so I assumed he'd moved on to another room. I popped the pills in my mouth, took a big swallow of water from the glass I brought in with me, and I found him – in the glass – floating. They say in moments of near death, your life passes before your eyes. I didn't see scenes from my six-plus decades on this earth, but a number of thoughts chased each other across my mind in the next nanosecond as I leaned over the sink poised to spit.

- *Oh gross! No telling what's in my mouth.*
- *Well, aside from anything else, there are two pills. If I spit, they'll go down the sink.*
- *One is a calcium supplement that I got for free with a coupon from my Medicare Part D carrier, but when they're gone, I'll have to buy more.*
- *One is a timed-release niacin supplement that cost $50 a bottle. I don't have time to calculate how much that is per pill, but I really don't want to waste one.*
- *I don't feel anything wiggling around in my mouth. Maybe I missed all the bug parts.*

In the end, I swallowed quickly and tried not to think about what I might have ingested. I poured the remaining contents of the glass into the sink, averting my eyes as the bug swirled down the drain. I didn't want to know if anything was missing.

So that's my bug adventures for the week. I'm probably suffering from some mild post traumatic stress, but in the end, I came out the winner.

CHAPTER 8

I Love Trees – Sometimes – 7/6/14

Several years ago, David and I needed a place to move the mobile home he lived in before we were married. Our wish list for the perfect piece of land was simple - trees, water, and a very small price tag. That list wasn't so simple in the area north of Dallas where our search began, so we eventually ended up working with a realtor in Rains County. Some would say it was good fortune, but I prefer to think it was a bit of divine intervention that led us to a two-acre lot that was affordable and had a tiny creek delineating the northern property line. Best of all, it had eighty-five trees.

We loved those trees, especially in the Spring when all the tiny buds began to appear on the winter-bare limbs followed by the fresh, delicate new greenery that no artist can adequately duplicate. We continued to love them until Fall came. Eighty-five trees produce a lot of leaves! David likes to burn, though, and the lawn mower chewed up a lot of dry foliage.

Then the drought got worse, and some of our red oaks went from distressed to dead. It became a little harder to hold on to the love when we had to pay to remove tree skeletons that threatened to drop their bony limbs on the house, the shed, the motor home, the car, or the motorcycle. The positive aspect of the removal was the stumps - more excuses for David to start fires.

We haven't lost as many whole trees in the last couples of years, but a large number have a limb or two that have succumbed to the dry weather or the powdery fungus that has infected many of the trees in the area. As a result, our yard has become a hard-hat zone. We take our lives in our hands every time we walk from the house to the creek, never knowing when a dead branch will let go of its trunk and throw itself to the ground.

We discovered last week that the house is not safe either. I was working in the kitchen on the Fourth when I heard a huge crash. I rushed outside, fearing I'd find David flattened under a length of dead wood. Instead I found a large branch that had hit the ground and bounced into a bedroom window. The window lost the fight.

I still love the trees, especially in the Spring. I even enjoy the smell of burning leaves in the Fall. However, there are moments when I think back longingly of that nice, flat, treeless lot just south of town.

CHAPTER 9

Country Girls Have Septic Tanks – 3/7/15

We were late to home group Bible study Friday night. David had to take a last minute shower because he had been playing in the septic tank. That's something I never said when I lived in the city.

The truth is, until we moved to Emory, I knew very little about septic tanks. I knew they were a few steps above an outhouse on the sewage evolutionary scale, but that's about it. In Florida, you could tell if a house had a septic tank because it was under a large mound of earth that must have been a real challenge to mow. That's probably because it was only half buried in order to remain above the water table, but that's just an uneducated guess. Septic tanks are also the basis for some interesting stories.

My aunt has been a widow for over a decade and lives alone on a farm west of Sulphur Springs. Although she is very independent, some of her neighbors think she sometimes needs to be protected. One night during a terrible storm, one such neighbor drove into her yard and made a mad dash through her back door.

"Ms. Fay, come on over to our house and stay in our safe room with us!" she shouted above the driving rain and wind.

"No, thank you! I'm fine right here," replied Aunt Fay. "You need to get home and be with your husband, and you need to get your car off the top of my septic tank!"

Our pastor also has a septic tank story. He was once doing a series on church elders - on their biblical precedence, their qualifications, and their duties. He said that elders would be called on to perform many of the same duties as a pastor, and he gave some illustrations from his own ministry experience. One example involved dipping out a septic tank with a coffee can. I didn't feel like it was a particularly motivational story.

I guess David felt differently, though. Friday afternoon, I looked out the window and saw him using a bucket to bail water out of our tank. I guess I should say "tanks," since we have an aerobic system that includes three of them. Our system is in the lowest spot in our yard, and with all the runoff from the recent precipitation, frozen and otherwise, all three tanks were full. It was a circular kind of problem. The tanks were full because the sprinkler pump wasn't working properly, and the pump wasn't working properly because it was under water - because the tanks were full.

So, that's why David was playing in the septic tank, why he had to take a last minute shower, and why we were late to Bible study. It's not an excuse we've had to offer before, and we hope not to have to offer it again. At any rate, the other members of the group were grateful we were late.

CHAPTER 10

Lessons from the Storm – 4/26/15

Friday night's storm left its mark on the Brendle homestead. When we looked out the windows Saturday morning, we saw several fallen limbs and more standing water than most Texas homeowners see unless a water line has sprung a leak. After breakfast, David went to check out the damage. A few minutes later he stuck his head in the front door.

"Your garden took quite a beating last night," he said. "Most of the corn and a lot of the tomatoes are down, and the water broke through one of your rows and washed out a garlic plant."

I sighed, shut down my computer, and changed into my gardening clothes. I knew I would need rubber boots, but since I don't have any, I had to settle for tennis shoes. I know that's not what they're called now, but I can't tell a cross-trainer from a walking shoe.

I sloshed through the grass and spent the next couple of hours playing in the mud. I wiped off the leaves of tiny seedlings that were stuck in the dirt, I removed the broken shoots from the tomato plants and staked up the stems, I packed mud around the exposed roots of the corn, and I worked on pulling the multitude of weeds that seemed to survive the storm quite nicely. While I worked, I thought a lot about water.

A couple of weeks ago, we had water night at AWANA. Keeping with the same theme, we talked about living water the next week during story time. We talked about John 7:38 where Jesus said that anyone who believed in Him would have rivers of living water flowing from within them. As I pulled the weeds that came up easily out of the saturated ground, I thought about how much easier it is to keep the "weeds" out of our lives when we keep ourselves saturated with living water.

While I was working and musing in the garden, David was playing in the septic tank again. I wrote a few weeks ago about how our aerobic system flooded during the rain, and he had to bail out the excess water in order to get the sprinklers to run. If the sprinklers don't keep the water level down, the aerator pump won't run, and the whole system is useless. Saturday, he pulled out enough water to expose the pump, but the system still wouldn't come on. He came over to check on my progress, and we agreed it was time to call it a day. Always the optimist, though, he decided to give the sprinklers one more try before we went in for lunch. I watched him walk down to the electrical control panel, and as he leaned over to hit the reset button, I whispered a little prayer.

"He's worked so hard. Please let it start."

I heard a little voice inside my head whisper back. *You'd better get out of the way.* I looked down and realized I was standing almost on top of one of the sprinkler heads. I made it to the porch just as the head popped up and a fifteen-foot stream of water spewed out. Mom always told me you sometimes have to put feet to your prayers.

Country life isn't always easy. There are times when I think it would simplify our lives if we rented a permanent spot at an RV campground and lived in the motor home. True, it might be easier, but it wouldn't be nearly as educational.

CHAPTER 11

In Danger of Losing My Identity – 5/23/15

I may be in danger of losing my identity as a city girl. Last week David and I drove into the city, and I didn't like it very much – at least the city part of it.

In February, the winter weather prevented some of our friends from the Dallas area from coming to Emory for my first book signing. Two absentees were Peggy and James, the former neighbors and motorcycle buddies who play several pivotal roles in my book. Even though we hadn't seen each other since 2007 when we came through the Metroplex in our RV, Peggy and I have kept in touch by email and Facebook. Disappointed by the lost opportunity to reconnect at the signing, we devised another plan - she invited me to speak at an upcoming Sunday school dinner. As the time drew closer, James suggested that we spend the night so we could have more time to catch up.

Last Monday, we left Emory shortly after lunch to drive the ninety miles to Carrollton for the planned event and visit. David decided to avoid the major highways and stick to the back roads like Highways 380 and 121. Imagine how shocked we were at the changes the years had brought - the commercial and residential buildings where there had been open fields; the major intersections and traffic lights instead of long uninterrupted straight-aways; and the traffic.

Our neighborhood was always a quiet island in the middle of a sea of commerce, but the growing maze of fast-food eateries, gas stations, and stores that now encircled it was overwhelming. Still, the residential streets were quite, shielded from the surrounding chaos by hedges and brick walls. I hadn't realized how tense I was until I began to relax as we drove down the familiar streets. I felt a tug of homesickness as we passed our old home, but it eased when James welcomed us into their home next door.

We arrived mid-afternoon, so we had several hours to visit before we had to leave for dinner. The class was meeting at Anamia's, a Tex-Mex restaurant in Plano - a thirty-minute ride back through the traffic. Thankfully, James was driving, so we could enjoy the conversation that continued non-stop.

Dinner was delicious, and my presentation went well. In addition to reading a section from my book, I talked about keeping your marriage strong while caregiving. I could tell by the reactions of my small audience that I was talking about an issue that touched many of their lives. I sold a few books, but more importantly, I think my experiences encouraged some of the people who were going through similar circumstances.

When we got back to our home for the night, the four of us talked until midnight, sharing what had happened while we had been separated by hundreds of miles and several states. The visit continued the next morning, but after lunch, it was time for David and me to leave the city. He negotiated the traffic with a little less surprise but no less tension than the day before, and we were glad when we were able to slip back into the slower pace of Rains County.

When we arrived home, I unpacked my overnight bag and headed for the kitchen where I enjoyed the view that included lots of trees and a few energetic squirrels.

After we ate, the darkness that comes when there are no big city lights around was still a couple of hours away, so I went out to the garden for a while. I spent some time pulling weeds, adjusting support stakes to accommodate new growth, and otherwise tending to plants that not too long ago were a mystery to me. While I puttered, I mulled over the changes that have occurred in my life in the last few years. I realized that, instead of being a total city girl, I now feel more at home when I have a little bit of dirt under my fingernails.

CHAPTER 12

Can you cut up a chicken? – 9/7/15

Ideas came easily the last two weeks. All I had to do was recount the antics of Spike, the mischievous pet we were staying with while his "parents" were out of town. Both columns were written and submitted on Saturday, well before the Monday morning deadline. Not so this week. When I turned on my computer after lunch on Sunday, I had a bad case of writer's block. I played several games of Free Cell, Mahjong, and Spider Solitaire while I waited for inspiration, but as dinner time approached, my word document was still blank.

I finally resorted to a modern resource - Facebook - where I posted the following status update: *I have a City Girl column due for this week's paper without a clue what to write about. Suggestions?* I received a few responses, but the first one caught my attention. *As I was standing at the sink cutting chicken wings apart to make some hot wings, I started thinking about how many chickens I have cut up and fried during my lifetime. Do any of you young girls cut up a whole chicken for frying? My daughter is a fabulous cook, but she wouldn't have a clue how to cut up a chicken! You young ones weigh in on this...I'm thinking I may have become antique!*

Apparently home-cooked fried chicken is becoming a thing of the past. She received thirty responses, the majority from people who had never cut up a whole chicken and who had never even fried one.

I learned to cook when I was eleven years old. We lived in Mesquite, Mom worked in Dallas, and it was 6:30 by the time she made it home each evening. I volunteered to add dinner to my household chores, and with lots of instructions, I could soon put a simple meal on the table. With practice, I increased my skill and my menus, and I eventually learned to dissect and fry a decent chicken.

Then I married, and my new family preferred hamburgers and hot dogs to fried chicken. Over time, I grew lazy, and the grocery stores began to market chicken pieces in addition to whole birds. When chicken was on the menu, I bought breasts and cooked them on the grill.

David's tastes are much broader though, so now I occasionally buy legs and thighs, but I still don't fry. I actually bought a whole chicken recently, but I cooked it whole in the crock pot. It was tasty, but it was so tender I had to remove it from the pot in pieces with a spoon.

Today's general lack of homemade fried chicken is more than replaced by the many commercial eateries that specialize in the delicacy. Still, they serve breasts, thighs, and legs, and in some cases, various flavors of wings. When I used to cut up chickens, there were other pieces. My favorite was the wish bone, better known in my house as the pulley bone. Mom liked what she called the side boards, now sometimes included as a part of a split breast and called the rib meat. There was also a back and a tail piece. I don't really miss any of those pieces except maybe the pulley bone, but I sometimes wonder what happens to them after the rest of the chicken is packaged and on the way to market.

Some pet foods list chicken by-products on the ingredients list. In addition, lots of chicken sausages, hot dogs, and sandwich meats are now on the market. Maybe I'll quit asking questions. Sometimes it's better not to know.

GARDENING

CHAPTER 13

I Planted a Scraggly Garden – 5/27/12

I planted a garden a couple of weeks ago. It's not the garden I envisioned earlier in the year. Now that we've removed several trees, we have some perfect garden spots that get full sun, and David's mom has a tiller she has offered to give us. In February I imagined a large area, tilled and mulched and fertilized, ready for several rows of squash and okra and beans, all those things that are so good for you but are so expensive in the grocery store. Then we began to make tentative plans to visit Florida for a month or so this summer, so I watched with envy as neighbors laid out their garden plots and tended the tiny green plants that stretched toward the warm Texas sun. But plans don't always work out, and we realized that the trip to Florida isn't going to happen, so when we went to Hooten's to get some oil for the chain saw, I asked David a question.

"Is it too late to plant tomatoes?"

Remember, I'm a city girl. True, I'm only one generation removed from the fields of West Texas, but it was a pretty complete removal. Mom and Dad were both raised on farms, but Mom never liked it. Her sisters called her their house cat, because she would swap chores with anyone to avoid working outside. She wanted to get away from the farm as quickly as possible and never had a desire to return. She enjoyed fresh corn, peas, and cantaloupe when they were in season, but she wanted to buy them at the produce stand and prepare and eat them in the air-conditioned comfort of home. The only exposure I had to gardening was at Aunt Fay's. She and Uncle Dean always had a sizeable plot full of all sorts of good things to eat, but Mom made sure we weren't around during planting and harvesting time.

Despite Mom's best efforts, my country girl genes creep through from time to time. When I was single again, I tried to raise a couple of tomato plants on the patio of my tiny, zero-lot-line home. One Saturday morning I checked on my babies and was dismayed at their condition. Half the leaves were gone, and many of the remaining ones were full of holes. Dad was still in good health and came over on the weekends to help me with my yard work.

"Dad, come look at my tomatoes. What's wrong with them!"

"You've got tomato worms," he said as he pulled one of the fat, green critters from one of the stems and squashed it with his shoe.

"Ewww, gross!" I'm not that much of a country girl.

With the help of a little chemical spray and a vigilant eye, my scraggly plants survived. I have to admit that I didn't adopt Dad's method of dealing with the worms. If I found one, I snipped off the whole stem and threw it away. In spite of the worms and my squeamishness, I produced a few scrawny, misshapen tomatoes with tough skins.

"Cool," said Christian when he saw my crop. "Can I have them to make salsa!"

It's nice to have your efforts appreciated.

A few years later after David and I married, we planted some tomatoes and peppers in a flower bed in the back yard. The peppers grew nicely, producing pods so hot that even David couldn't eat a whole one. The tomatoes didn't do so well. They were doing okay, but I left them on the vine a little too long. The morning I went out to harvest them, some critter had taken a bite out of the bottom of each one.

So it was with this limited experience and questionable success that I asked David about the tomatoes in Hooten's.

"I don't think it's too late," he said.

I dragged him out to the garden section to see what they had. The selection was very limited, but I found a couple of promising looking tomato plants, a four-pack of cayenne peppers, and another four-pack of Anaheim peppers. Not the wide variety I originally planned, but enough to play with and not enough to feel like I threw away a lot of money if my results are less than stellar.

The next morning I put on my working-in-the-yard hat and gloves and went out to bed down my plants. I chose a sunny, weed-free area and started digging. We haven't made it to Louisiana to get the tiller yet; it would have been overkill for such a small plot anyway. The sandy soil is nice and loose, so I dug ten small holes and worked in a little bit of soil from a compost pile left by a previous resident. I mixed up a bucket of plant food and gave them all a good soaking. Finally, I marked the corners of the plot with four large rocks so my Cub Cadet pilot won't run over my babies by mistake, or maybe on purpose. David laughed and said my little plot looks a little scraggly.

He's right. It's a little scraggly, and I don't know what will happen. Some people are predicting another hot, dry summer, so it may all burn up before it has a chance to produce. Or the critters may get into it. If they do, maybe they'll leave me enough for a batch of salsa and a pot of green chili stew. Regardless, I'm looking forward to watching the process. I think watching a tiny plant take dirt, water, and sunshine and turn it into something good to eat is nothing short of a miracle. It's like being present at the Creation: "Let there be...and there was...and it was good."

CHAPTER 14

Return on Investment - Plant the Seeds and Watch the Increase – 10/7/12

I made a pot of green chili stew last week using home grown Anaheim peppers. In May I planted a small garden: 2 tomato plants, 4 cayenne peppers and 4 Anaheim peppers. David laughed and said it looked a little scraggly. He was right, but the squirrels didn't mind. They watched carefully, and every time a tomato got about the size of a ping pong ball, they carefully snatched it, leaving no broken leaves or incriminating paw prints. I don't know how many I lost; I quit counting after 30.

The squirrels didn't like the peppers though, and I got several dozen Anaheims. I used a few in cooking as I picked them, but I roasted most of them and put them in the freezer in anticipation of stew season. I also got lots of cayennes. I used jalapenos from my aunt's garden to make salsa, but I used some of my cayennes to make hot pepper relish and hot vinegar. David is eating most of the rest of them raw, one or two with each meal. I think he'd even eat one for breakfast if I put them on the table.

Encouraged by my success, I planted some purple hull peas in August. I guess squirrels don't like peas either, because some of the pods started to mature a few days ago. I pick a few each day as the shells start to thin out and the tips begin to turn purple. A few more days and I'll have a pretty good mess – that Texan for enough to cook for dinner.

Several years ago when we still lived in Florida, I was pretty active in the stock market. I thought I was pretty hot stuff. I knew how to buy and sell, how place several kinds of stop losses, how to sell options against my positions. I was doing really well, and my 401K was growing to fairly impressive proportions. But then I got laid off, and we started having to draw funds from my account to cover living expenses. I held my own for a while, but then the market got really crazy. Anybody with a little bit of knowledge and the nerve to hit the buy or sell button once in a while can make money in an up market, but it takes some real expertise to make money when the charts look like a roller coaster. I didn't have that kind of expertise, and before long my small gains couldn't keep up with the withdrawals. When we moved back to Texas, our limited internet access made it almost impossible to follow the market, so I retired from trading. I still have a few shares of a couple of old favorites, and I have one share of Google I got when one of the companies whose stock I held was bought out, but my account sits idle, and I hope for slow and steady growth.

Even at my most successful, my trading return on investment was nothing compared to what I've seen in my garden. It's true that my tomatoes were a total loss unless you count a few happy squirrels, but my peppers more than made up the difference. Each Anaheim plant produced at least 2 dozen peppers, and the cayennes more than doubled that yield. I planted 60 purple hull peas (yes, I counted, and yes, I may have a slight case of OCD), and I've already harvested almost a cupful. I haven't counted, but that's probably 5 or 6 times as many as I planted in a little less than two months. If I had made that kind of profit in the market, we'd be rolling down the highway in a brand new motorhome!

Jesus liked good returns on investments, too. In the parable of the talents, he told about two faithful servants who were praised for doubling the money that had been entrusted to them. But in the parable of the seeds, he talked about a much greater return:

As for what was sown on good soil, this is the one who hears the word and understands it. He indeed bears fruit and yields, in one case a hundredfold, in another sixty, and in another thirty. Matthew 13:23

I love watching my little garden seeds germinate and produce fruit that far exceeds my expectations. It's even more exciting to watch the seeds that God plants come to fruition. When verses come to mind while I'm writing, I always try to use them. He might be planting a seed, and who knows what kind of return on investment He has in mind.

CHAPTER 15

Success Is a Two-Inch Tomato! – 11/29/12

I've written several articles about my little garden in the past few months. Gardens are not very exciting to those who've grown them all their lives, but they're nothing short of miraculous to a city girl whose previous horticultural experiences consists of a window sill herb garden and a few pots of patio tomatoes. Every time I take a bag of frozen squash or okra from the freezer or open a jar of salsa or pickled okra, I think *this isn't the product of a giant faceless corporation. This is the result of hard work by Aunt Fay, Jerry, Dirk and even me.*

Yes, even my scraggly little garden has been a success. I wrote about my crop of Anaheim and cayenne peppers along with my late crop of black-eyed peas. I also wrote about my tomatoes, all of which had been stolen well before they reached maturity by some tricky varmint I could never catch in the act. I thought my plants had done their thing for the season, and I was about to plow them under, or at least shovel them under, in preparation for next year.

Then Indian Summer came, and my tomato plants, misshapen and propped up as they were, began to bloom again. Hope springs eternal, so I left them alone and waited to see what would happen. The blooms set, and little tomatoes started to pop out. I guess the varmints were busy with acorns and other Fall offerings, because all but two of the tiny green balls stayed on the vine. When the nights turned cool, I covered the aged plants and uncovered them during the day so they could catch a few rays. And it finally happened – one of them ripened! It's only about two inches in diameter, and it's split in a couple of places, but it feels like success. The rest of the tomatoes have stayed green, and they haven't grown much. I'll probably strip them off in the next day or two and make a very small batch of green tomato relish or stir-fry them with some other veggies.

I'm excited by my success, and I'm planning for next year. In fact, I've already started. Dirk Schutter, the neighbor who gave me the monster zucchini earlier in the year, is also the garlic king of the neighborhood. If he has anything to do with it, there will never be any vampires in Rains County. He has supplied me with huge, flavorful cloves of garlic all season, and he gave me twenty bulbs to start a crop of my own. At his direction, I planted them last month, and all of them have come up. I'm expecting a great harvest in March.

I saved squash and zucchini seeds from gifts given to me by Dirk and Aunt Fay, and I have watermelon and cantaloupe seeds from Jerry Parrish, another neighbor. Jerry said he also has okra seeds if I need them. He told me to watch for onion sets in the stores in February or March, and I'll try to get my tomatoes in the ground early, maybe before the squirrels run out of their winter stash of nuts and start shopping in the local gardens. Ronnie Brown, our next-door-neighbor, cut down a tree that was shading part of my garden area, so now I have plenty of room to expand. I'm excited about my prospects. Others are looking forward to the Christmas season, but I'm looking past that to the growing season.

Wish me luck, and when things start to ripen, you might want to watch out if you see me walking down the street. I might be carrying a bag of zucchini I'm trying to give away!

CHAPTER 16

Plans, God, and Day Lilies – 3/24/13

Proverbs 16:9 says *The heart of man plans his way, but the Lord establishes his steps.* The Yiddish version is something like "Man plans and God laughs." I wonder if God laughed last Friday when I thought the day's plans might include a little writing.

I knew I wouldn't get any writing done in the morning. I had some homework to do for the ladies' Bible study we're having at church, and I needed to do a little work in the garden. I got the homework done, but then I checked my e-mails, and before I knew it, it was time to go to the Senior Center. That was okay. There would be time for gardening when we got back from lunch with time left over to come up with a brilliant article and spend some time on the book I'm working on.

I got a late start with my gardening last year, so I was determined to get a head start this year. In fact, I started in October by planting the garlic bulbs Dirk, a generous neighbor, gave me. All the bulbs came up, and they should be ready to harvest soon. I put in early onions that seem to be doing well, and some spinach and carrot seeds have come up. I jumped the gun with some bedding plants, and although my broccoli plants are thriving, I've lost two red cabbages and most of my lettuce. The jury's still out on whether the potatoes will come up. I've got lots of other things to plant, and since I'm working with hand tools, it's a time consuming hobby.

But I'm excited about it, and all my friends who have gardened all their lives seem to get a kick out of the city girl getting her fingernails dirty. They've all become enablers of my new habit. I've been given lots of advice and two dried pods of okra seeds - a gift only a gardener would love. And now I'm getting flowers. A couple of weeks ago we saw Dirk and his wife Pat working in the yard and stopped to chat.

"Hey, Linda," he said, leaning in the car window. "Do you want some white irises?"

"Sure, if you've got some you're getting rid of. And if you thin out those day lilies, I'll take any you have left over."

So I left with a box of irises and a job ahead of me. When you buy bedding plants from a nursery, you have a few days before you have to get them in the ground. Not so with neighbor-to-neighbor transfers. After an hour jammed into a cardboard box, my irises were beginning to look a little distressed. The clumps of sandy soil were falling apart, leaving the rhizomes and roots exposed and the leaves were looking a little thirsty. Any attempt to add water would have resulted in a soggy mess, so I had no choice but to get them in the ground.

It was hard work. David was busy on the mower, so I had to do the whole job, from digging out the bed to watering in the new plants. I was so sore I could hardly move the next day, but it was worth it. We will now have some white blooms to go along with the purple vinca I planted last year. And we solved a mystery. When David saw the irises, they looked familiar to him.

"I think we already have some of those."

"Oh, really," I said. "Where?"

"Several places around the yard. I've just been mowing them down."

I guess that's why they haven't bloomed. One bunch has escaped the blade this spring. They're in a circle around what used to be a tree. It could be the beginning of a nice bed if not for the unfortunate placement right in front of where we park the motor home.

But back to last Friday. Dirk and I were talking dirt again at the Senior Center.

"Linda, if you want some day lilies, you need to get them pretty soon. They're the perfect size for transplanting."

David and I had plans the next couple of days, and there was rain in the forecast, so when I got home, instead of sitting down at the computer, I donned my gardening clothes and headed over to Dirk's. I ended up with another box of fragile root systems to care for, and I still had some bare spots in my vegetable garden to re-seed. I'm not one of those Martha Stewart kind of gardeners who can finish a day of planting and weeding and watering and still look cute and dainty and spotless. At the end of my sessions, I look like I've been rolling in the dirt. I have hat hair, my face is red from the heat, and my gloves are as dirty on the inside as on the outside. After the transplants and seeds were bedded, I needed a shower, and David and I were both ready for dinner.

By the time the dishes were done, it was dark outside, and instead of an insightful, thought-provoking article and a new chapter or two, I wrote the first edition of Linda's 2013 Almanac. I hope you enjoyed it as much as God did. He's laughing.

CHAPTER 17

From Trash to Watermelons – 4/13/13

When we bought our little two-plus acre homestead four years ago, it was in need of some TLC. Among other things, there were piles of junk and partially burned trash all over the place. In particular, there was a large pile covered by a huge log. The downed tree was blackened and surrounded by a mound of dirt and the non-combustible remains of many fires.

We didn't have much time to devote to clearing it at the time. We were in Texas temporarily, just long enough to buy the property, move David's mobile home onto it, get rid of the worst of the debris and get the house ready for tenants. Then we returned to Florida and our caregiving duties.

When we moved back to Texas permanently two years ago, the pile was worse. The log was smaller from more fires, but the pile of trash around it had grown. The tree behind it on the left was dead, the evergreen on the right was still alive but was leaning at a sixty-degree angle, and the whole area was choked with weeds and briars. Our tenants weren't much into yard work.

Since then, we've done a lot of work. The dead and leaning trees are gone, and a storage shed sits to the left of the pile. The log is long since gone, and the surrounding weeds are mostly under control, although David still has to spray the mound itself with weed killer from time to time. Most of the surface trash has been carted off, but every time we have a heavy rain or a strong wind, bits of broken glass and rusted metal surface. But all that changed earlier this week.

I got garden fever early this year, and I bought seeds - lots of seeds. I started with a small plot in a sunny spot close to the road. I filled up 5 rows, and then I moved to the area where I planted tomatoes and peppers last year. I expanded that little plot and filled it, but I still had seeds left - watermelon seeds - so I started looking for a likely spot. I don't know a lot about gardening, but I know watermelons grow best on a hill.

"David, do you think watermelons would grow on that trash mound?"

"I don't know if they'll like the ashes, but there's some pretty good dirt under there. It wouldn't hurt to try."

He's still fighting dead trees and poison ivy at the back of the lot, so I do most of the gardening. I got my grubbing hoe and my rake and went to work. It was a hard job. Even though the weeds were dead, there were lots of roots to dig up, and I filled up two five-gallon buckets with debris. I'm not as young as I used to be, and I'm about the get a year older, so it took me a couple of days to finish. I got the seeds planted Tuesday afternoon before the rain started that night. Now we'll just have to wait and see what happens.

Gardening requires more muscle power than brain power, so my mind wanders while I dig and weed and plant. Sometimes I think about trivia, but sometimes I think about spiritual things. The Bible talks a lot about seeds and growth and pruning, and I wondered if there was a parable or Scripture passage that went along with my efforts to produce watermelons from a trash pile. There are lots of stories about people whose lives were drastically changed for the better after a touch from Jesus, but nothing about watermelons. Then I thought about the fruits of the Spirit. In Galatians 5 the Apostle Paul tells the church in Galatia to clean up their act and start practicing the love that Jesus taught so their lives would produce love, joy, peace, patience, kindness, goodness, faithfulness, gentleness, and self-control. He doesn't specifically mention watermelons, but that's some pretty powerful fruit.

CHAPTER 18

Garlic Wars Escalate in Emory – 5/7/13

"You lost another garlic plant last night," said David yesterday after his morning inspection of the kingdom.

Simple words, but with earth-shaking consequences for the garlic monster that's taken a third plant. That's fifteen percent of my crop, and even God only asks for ten percent.

"Okay, no more Mrs. Nice Guy," I said. "We're going to Hooten's after lunch so I can talk to the garden guy."

It turned out to be his day off, and the man who was filling in (I'll call him Jim - not to protect his privacy but because I've forgotten his name) wasn't sure how to answer my questions.

"Something's eating my garlic from underground. Do you have any idea what it might be?"

"Hmmm. Maybe it's grubs."

"Do you really think so? Grubs would probably just gnaw at the bulb, wouldn't they? That's not what's happening. The plant starts to sag, and when I pull it up there's nothing there. It's as if the whole bulb of garlic has been harvested from the bottom, just cut off."

"Maybe it's moles or gophers."

Like most men, David doesn't like to ask for directions, and he doesn't like to ask for help in a store. While I was having this conversation, he was doing a search on the little problem-solving computer halfway down the aisle.

"It says moles eat grubs and worms and such, but gophers eat bulbs and other plants. Sounds like it's a gopher to me."

Jim seemed relieved to have some direction, so he showed me the options for eliminating my problem. I picked up an electronic device that supposedly drives pests away with a high-pitched tone that's inaudible to humans. It sounded nice and clean and humane. Unfortunately, it was intended mostly for mice, and it had to be plugged into an electrical outlet. My garden is much improved over last year, but it's not yet supplied with electricity, so we moved on to more primitive methods.

He showed me a cone-shaped container of poison that claimed the power to rid me of the furry monster in a more permanent way. Then he showed me a gopher trap. It was a small but complicated metal gizmo made up of various springs and triggers and some very evil looking spiky things. He set it gingerly, making sure it didn't snap back on his fingers. He almost used his knife to trip the trigger and show me how it worked, but he considered the possible effects on his fingers and thought better of it. He found an open flat space, set the trap down and used a long rod to set it off. When he hit the release and the evil-looking sides snapped together, I turned and reached for the poison.

"I think I'll try this," I said.

I think I can deal with the thought of the garlic monster clutching his little throat, gasping for breath more easily than I can deal with the picture of him skewered in a contraption fit for the Marquis de Sade's chamber of horrors. I know it's war, but there are limits to what I'll do to protect my crops.

CHAPTER 19

Preemptive Harvest Ends Garlic Wars – 5/23/13

Earlier this month I wrote an article about the Garlic Wars being waged in my garden. An unknown enemy was making underground raids and eating my garlic from the bottom. I've had several people ask how it's going, so here's the latest.

After our trip to Hooten's for weapons, we prepared to engage in chemical warfare. Following the directions on the package, David poked around the affected area until he found several tunnels. He made holes about an inch in diameter and waited. If it was an active tunnel, the gopher or whatever little monster was eating my garlic was supposed to repair the hole within 24 hours. David went out every morning to check the holes, but none of them were ever repaired. Apparently the gopher had read the package direction, too. And the garlic continued to disappear. A fourth one bit the dust, and when a fifth one keeled over, I gave up.

"That's it. He's taken a fourth of my crop. I'm going to pull it all up even if it's a little early."

"Okay," said David, "but I think I'll go ahead and put out some poison anyway. From the looks of this mound, he may be headed toward your carrots."

I wasn't too disappointed in my yield. I got 15 very large bulbs which should be more than enough to keep the vampires away until next season.

The rest of my garden is doing well. The zucchini is blooming like crazy, and several little yellow squash have popped out. The cucumbers are a little behind, but I saw a bloom on one of those yesterday.

The watermelon seeds I planted in the old trash pile have come up and seem to be doing nicely. I hope the deer stay out of them.

My tomatoes are coming on beautifully. One of my internet friends read about my problem last year with the squirrels taking all my tomatoes and suggested that I use cayenne pepper to keep them away. Aunt Fay says that will just spice up the tomatoes for them, but I'm trying it anyway. It's worked so far.

I did a little more harvesting today. I was weeding around the potatoes and saw what I thought was a mushroom growing beside one of the stems. I reached over and flicked it away, and it was a little new potato. Since I had one, I dug around and found a few more for dinner. The tops of the carrots are getting pretty tall, so I pulled a few of those, too. They're a little gnarly looking - may not have tilled deep enough - but they'll be good in a salad.

By the time I finished all that, I was ready for a shower. I'm beginning to feel like I know a little bit about what I'm doing, but I still manage to get filthy, regardless of how much protective clothing I wear. As I gathered my tools, I scanned the garden one more time and realized the war may be heating up on another front. One of my onions is missing.

CHAPTER 20

Am I Smarter Than a Fifth Grader? – 6/18/13

No, I'm not even smarter than the local squirrels.

Last year I wrote (and whined) a lot about the squirrels who were stealing my tomatoes. I had two little plants and was so proud when the little green fruit started to show up. But one by one, before any of them could get larger than a golf ball, they disappeared. After searching the internet and picking the brain of every experienced gardener I knew, I narrowed down the usual suspects to squirrels. I went to the local hardware/lumber/garden/everything store where the resident expert sold me some pellets that were supposed to repel all comers, but the tomatoes continued to disappear.

As the season drew to a close, I finally picked a 2" red tomato that was disappointingly tasteless and a handful of green tomatoes that I breaded in Louisiana Fish Fry and soaked in hot grease until they were a beautiful golden brown. They upset my stomach. A less than stellar season, but my cayenne and Anaheim peppers were successful enough to encourage me to try again this year.

I started well enough. I lost 2 of 12 tomato plants within the first couple of days, but the remaining 10 thrived and bloomed. I staked and fed and watered, and the tomatoes came. And they stayed – for a while. I guess the squirrels were still working on their winter stash of acorns. Then the tomatoes started to disappear. One or two at first, so I wasn't completely sure any were missing. Then the thief got bolder, taking more and leaving no doubt of his crime.

I didn't waste any time. I went straight to Hooten's, bought some netting, hammered "tent" stakes into the ground, and draped the endangered plants. It worked – for a while.

Sunday morning we came home from church and there was a squirrel – inside the tent – chomping on a big green tomato. Needless to say, I wasn't pleased. I screamed and stomped and the squirrel went ballistic, dodging between rows of tomatoes, trying to find an exit. After he made his getaway, I found the weakness and fortified the perimeter.

After dinner, I went out to water. There, sitting on one of the boards that secured the netting to the ground, was my biggest tomato with four bit bites out of the top of it. That little furry-tailed rat was taunting me! I closed the gaps again the best I could and went in the house and cried on David's shoulder.

Obviously we needed more netting. The plants and their supporting stakes were tall enough that there wasn't enough material left to secure it to the ground properly. Monday morning we went out to rearrange what we had in a way that would protect the plants until we could get to the store.

All was well when we left for lunch, but we stayed at the Center longer than usual, and of course, we had to stop at Hooten's on the way home. We got home around 4:00 pm, and the first thing I saw when we pulled into the driveway was a half-eaten tomato lying about 10 feet from the garden. Several smaller victims lay scattered inside the tent, and the center plant was lying on its side.

I sighed in resignation and went inside to fix dinner. David reassured me that the raids were probably over for the day and promised to help me construct a new shelter first thing Tuesday morning.

It wasn't a graceful undertaking. The pieces of net are 14'x14', and they kept snagging on the support poles which are mostly thin branches taken from the dead trees David has been cutting down. In addition, we had to be careful not to step on the row of peppers on one side and the row of okra on the other. We finally managed to remove the original netting, shore up the sagging stakes and plants, and reconstruct the tent. There was plenty of surplus material on the ground, and we secured the circumference with end-to-end rocks and boards, double stacking in areas that looked a little vulnerable. We poked and prodded to check for weaknesses and left for lunch feeling confident that our crop was safe.

What can I say? The squirrel is smarter than we are. When we got home, there was half of a larger green tomato sitting right in the middle of the tomato patch. It was the ultimate locked door mystery. We poked and prodded some more and couldn't find anywhere he could have gotten in or out. David checked later and said there was a place where the two pieces of netting overlapped by several feet. He said it was possible the squirrel had made his way down the "corridor" between the two and come back out the same way. David closed the gap and, although he hasn't carried through yet, threatened to pull up a chair and guard the garden with his pellet gun.

The good thing is that the tomatoes are prolific and, in spite of the pilferage, there are lots left. Maybe the squirrel will take pity and leave us a few. All I want is enough for a nice salad, maybe a sandwich or two, and a couple of jars of salsa. Is that too much to ask?

CHAPTER 21

What I Did This Summer – 9/06/13

The City Girl has been out of touch for a couple of months, so a back-to-school essay seemed like a good idea. In the spring I wrote about fighting gophers for my garlic and onions and squirrels for my tomatoes, and then things got really busy.

In early June we went to Portland to visit our grandkids. We visited their parents a bit, too, but we grandparents have to keep our priorities in order. We did little things like playing games, reading bedtime stories, and going for walks. We also did some bigger things like planting a garden with 4-year-old Zoe, building a miniature golf course out of cardboard boxes with 9-year-old Mattias, and putting together an above-ground swimming pool with two frazzled parents. But mostly we smiled and hugged a lot.

When we got home, there were weeds and more squirrels and a fungus that attacked my squash, zucchini, and cucumbers. The carrots and potatoes did pretty well, though, and all of it together meant more time outside and less time at the keyboard.

Then we decided to go to camp. A couple in our church works for Our Father's Children, an organization that provides camping and mentoring opportunities for foster children, most of whom have been abused. There are two camps in this area each summer for 6 to 12 year olds, and since they try to keep the camper to counselor ratio at 2 to 1, volunteers are always needed. After checking out the details and doing some soul searching, David and I went through counselor training, and in late July we were off to Royal Family Kids Camp.

We swam and made crafts and went to Chapel. There was a huge slip and slide that stretched 100 yards down a hill, and Wednesday night there was a mega-birthday party for everyone. On Thursday the girls attended a Princess Tea Party dressed in formal attire and tiaras, and the boys went to True North where they did guy things and received personal blessings from their counselors. It was exhausting, but we loved every minute of it except for Friday when we had to say a teary good-bye to the children we had come to love. And there was the part where I broke my ankle.

It wasn't a dramatic incident. I managed to run relay races with my girls and ride the zip-line into the pond without doing myself any bodily harm. Then Tuesday night on the way back to the dorm, I slipped off a 3-inch curb and ended up in an ungraceful pile on the ground. My ankle immediately swelled up in protest, but the camp nurse and I agreed it was probably sprained. She wrapped it, and I hobbled through the rest of the week with the aid of pain relievers and ice packs.

When I got home, I visited my doctor just to be sure. At first he agreed that it was sprained, but X-rays showed a spiral fracture of the fibula. The orthopedist I saw next said nothing was out of place that needed surgery, so he fitted me with a contraption that looks and feels like a ski boot designed by the Marquis de Sade. Then he told me to go enjoy the rest of the summer.

It's hard to do much gardening when you can't bend and squat very well, so my weed-choked patch is pretty sad looking. The fungus finally got the cukes and the squash, and I guess the heat got the watermelons. I got one good mess of butter beans, but the grasshoppers made sure there wouldn't be a second picking. The good thing is that either the heat or David's expertise with a pellet rifle finally discouraged the squirrels, and we got some nice tomatoes.

The days are getting shorter now, and we've had a couple of almost pleasantly cool mornings recently. I have to wear my boot for another few weeks, but I'm getting the itch to plant again. David picked up his old garden tiller the last time we were in Louisiana, and if he can get it running, he can do the heavy work and I can at least drop in a few seeds. I'm putting the gophers and squirrels and grasshoppers on notice. I may be slow, but I'm back, and this boot packs a mighty mean stomp.

CHAPTER 22

Attention North Texas Gardeners - It's Time to Plant Onions – 1/28/14

I planted onions for the first time last year, but they didn't do all that well. I checked the Texas A&M website, and it said in the zone where I live to plant them between February 1 and March 1. Since it seems I'm always a little behind schedule, it was well into March before I got them in the ground.

I started with bulbs rather than plant sets, and all of them came up. I had nice green tops, but the onions themselves didn't develop very well. My resident gopher didn't help. When his continuous raids on my garlic forced me to harvest early, he turned his attentions to the onions. Once again, I harvested early to save what was left of my small crop. Small was the operative word. Most of the onions were tasty but less than an inch or two in diameter.

This year I have another chance. A couple of weeks ago a friend at the Senior Center came to lunch bearing gifts. She had purchased two bunches of onions sets – one red and one white – and since there were more than she could plant in her small backyard garden, she shared. I brought some home and set them on the island in the kitchen. They're still there. David asks frequently if I've planted my onions yet, and my friend at the Center has asked the same thing a time or two.

As if that weren't enough, a friend at church greeted me last week with this question: *Have you got your onions in yet?* I almost expect to hear a tiny knock on the door and to find that it's the gopher wanting to know where the onions are to go with the garlic I planted last fall. It's barely above freezing outside, and it's still January, but it seems that I'm already behind.

CHAPTER 23

Odd Beginnings Can Yield Beautiful Fruit – 2/26/14

Some people were still shoveling snow and scraping ice a couple of weeks ago when we had a Saturday that was sunny with a high of 73. It was a good day to be outside and to learn a valuable lesson about tomatoes and spiritual fruit.

As soon as we finished breakfast, David grabbed his tools and headed to the back of the lot where he's winning the war against years of fallen trees and tangled underbrush. With a little more cutting and a few more bonfires, we'll be able to see the creek bank all the way along the property line. I went outside, too, but I opted for the lighter duty of working in the garden. However, after five hours of weeding and planting, muscles that are more accustomed to sitting at a keyboard than bending and squatting are not sure it was such light duty.

I love digging in the dirt and then watching the miracle of new life breaking through into the sunshine and eventually producing something good to eat. I also love the freedom the manual work gives my mind to wander wherever it will. Saturday it wandered to Portland where my grandkids live. I thought about our visit last summer when we did a little gardening together. They had a collection of seeds from the happy meals of a local hamburger place, and I had brought a few seeds leftover from my planting. We found corners of the backyard flower beds that were perfect for sugar snap peas, spinach, carrots, and zucchini. Four-year-old Zoe was more interested in the project than nine-year-old Mattias. She pulled weeds, helped prepare the soil, planted seeds, and watered them in. His mind was on bigger projects like creating a miniature golf course with Grandpa David, but even he found a couple of minutes to drop in a few seeds.

I'm not sure how their garden did – probably not very well since I didn't hear much about it after we got home. But Mattias got involved in an interesting gardening project of his own a few weeks later. His mom Amy was preparing dinner one night, and as she was cutting a tomato for the salad, she discovered that some of the seeds had sprouted inside the tomato. She called Christian and the kids in to look at the oddity, and then she started to throw it away and look for one more suitable for dinner.

"Noooooo!" said Mattias. "You can't throw it away. We have to plant it!"

Christian and Amy tried to convince him that it was useless; that the sprout wouldn't grow. But Mattias was adamant.

"Okay," Christian said. "Go for it."

A couple of months later, Christian posted a picture on Facebook of Mattias holding a beautiful, ripe tomato produced by his odd little sprout.

While I dug in the dirt on Saturday, I thought about that tomato plant and wondered how often I'm like Amy and Christian, how often I ignore or dismiss someone because of beginnings that are unusual or that look unpromising. Do I overlook the potential in the difficult boy at AWANA who refuses to conform and perform on cue but then answers the questions with an understanding beyond his years? Do I dismiss the promise of a visitor who might be a valuable addition to our church family because she has tattoos or he has long, unkempt hair?

Jesus didn't overlook or dismiss those with unconventional or unacceptable beginnings; in fact, He sought them out. He stopped in the middle of the street, looked up, and invited himself to dinner with Zacchaeus, a notorious, cheating tax collector. He asked for a drink of water from a many-times-divorced Samaritan woman, someone that society said he should not acknowledge much less converse with. Mattias believed that those unusual tomato sprouts would produce something good, and Jesus knew that, with a touch from the Holy Spirit, new life can break through and even the most unusual beginnings can produce good fruit.

But the fruit of the Spirit is love, joy, peace, patience, kindness, goodness, faithfulness, gentleness, self-control; Galatians 5:22-23a

CHAPTER 24

Stewardship and Planting Trees – 4/27/14

The true meaning of life is to plant trees under whose shade you do not expect to sit. ~Nelson Henderson

I planted ten trees on Saturday - wannabe trees is really more accurate. Connie, one of my neighbors, is in tune with nature and interested in improving and preserving her surroundings. She frequently sends donations to the Arbor Day Foundation, and every time she does, she receives a thank you gift - trees. She apparently has all the trees she needs, or she doesn't think we have enough, because she passed her last gift on to me.

Looking at our almost two-and-a-half acre lot, the last thing you'd think we need is more trees. A couple of years ago, David took a tree census, and our population was eighty-five. We've lost a dozen or so to the drought since then, but we also have a lot of new saplings that the squirrels have planted. What we're lacking, though, is color. We have a couple of black gum trees that turn a beautiful red in the fall, and David uncovered four dogwoods when he was clearing brush at the back of the lot, but most of the others are red oaks and pin oaks with a few elms and cedar trees thrown in for variety. The trees Connie gave us are all flowering trees - two each of Sargent Crabapple, Eastern Redbud, Washington Hawthorn, White Flowering Dogwood, and Golden Raintree.

You would expect a package containing all those trees to be rather large, but not this one. This package was a long, thin bag made of heavy-duty plastic. Inside was a bundle of ten twigs ranging from twelve to eighteen inches in length, and each twig had tiny roots growing out of one end. The root ends were in a smaller plastic bag with some gel-like, moisture-retaining pellets. Even though I neglected this thoughtful gift for a couple of months, the roots were still wet, and some of the more ambitious twigs had sprouted tiny leaves.

I haven't planted many trees in my life, especially such embryonic ones, so I read the enclosed instructions. The first step was to remove the packing material, gently separate the roots, and soak them in a bucket of water for three to six hours. That gave me time to work on the next step - deciding where to plant them.

Connie had lots of suggestions about placement, but Feng Shui wasn't the only consideration. I didn't want them near the garden where they would block the sun, and David didn't want them in the middle where he would have to mow around them. Finding spots where the newcomers wouldn't be completely shaded by the veteran trees was also an issue. After walking the perimeter several times, I finally found ten spots that were at least acceptable and began the actual planting.

I enjoy working in the yard. Getting my hands dirty reminds me of the days when I played in the dirt with my brother and made mud pies with the other little girls in the neighborhood. Besides, the miracle of putting something in the ground and seeing it grow always inspires me. A session in the yard usually produces at least an article or two.

Saturday was no different. As I nestled the tiny twigs into their new homes, watered them in, and surrounded them with tomato cages to protect them from the mower, I wondered which ones would survive. I also wondered how long it would be before the survivors were big enough to bloom in the spring and give shade in the summer - and I wondered if we would still be here when that happens.

The first time I heard the quote by Nelson Henderson, my son Christian was talking about the trees in his front yard in Colorado. They were beautiful, but they were very old and beginning to show their age. He talked of plans to plant new trees between the older ones, so they could get good start before the older ones died. "That's my idea of stewardship," he said. "Planting trees you'll never sit under."

That's the way it is with a lot of things - charity, ministry, teaching, serving others. You do what needs to be done without knowing whether you'll get to see the results. The Apostle Paul put it this way in his first letter to the church in Corinth.

I planted, Apollos watered, but God gave the growth. So neither he who plants nor he who waters is anything, but only God who gives the growth. 1 Corinthians 3:6-7

CHAPTER 25

That Garden Will Preach – 5/31/14

One reason I love working in the garden is that, while my hands are busy, my mind is free to roam. Sometimes I focus on the latest song that's stuck in my head, and sometimes I think about a chapter in my next book or the next article I plan to write. My favorite times, though, are when God seems to open my mind and my heart to the spiritual lessons that can be found in the world around me. I spent last Saturday morning working my little vegetable patch, and here's what my garden taught me.

Strong roots will stand you in good stead.
Early in May, I bought nine small tomato plants and nestled them snugly into their bed. Since the squirrels don't usually start raiding until the actual tomatoes appear, I thought they would be safe until we returned from visiting David's mother for a week. Unfortunately, a rogue squirrel or a hungry rabbit made an unscheduled visit, and three tomato plants went missing while we were gone. I didn't pay much attention until last weekend when I went out to fight the

weeds. When I reached the tomato rows, I noticed that one of the little plants, although it had been gnawed down to the ground, was putting out new leaves. The unseen part of the plant had enough strength to survive what looked like a fatal blow and to come back strong.

Train up a child in the way he should go; even when he is old he will not depart from it. Proverbs 22:6

Bloom where you're planted.

As I reached the middle of the row, I saw something that I thought was a weed. On closer inspection, though, I discovered it was a tomato plant. The top of one of the ravaged plants had fallen off the small mound on which it was growing and landed in the low spot between rows. Undeterred, it had put down roots and was growing quite nicely.

12 I know how to be brought low, and I know how to abound. In any and every circumstance, I have learned the secret of facing plenty and hunger, abundance and need. 13 I can do all things through him who strengthens me. Philippians 4:12-13

Older plants – and older people – still have value.

After I finished with the tomatoes, I moved over to the "older" part of the garden where the mustard greens, spinach, and lettuce were. The leafy vegetables had gone to seed, and the bugs had begun to munch on the remaining leaves. It was time to remove the old plants and make room for some hot-weather crops. Sounds about like corporate America, doesn't it? Before I pulled anything up, though, I inspected carefully and harvested enough lettuce and spinach leaves for several salads. With all the edible parts salvaged, it was time to uproot--but it still wasn't time to discard. Through the weeks and months of sunshine, rain, and nutrients from the soil, these plants had stored up nourishment that could be passed on to the next generation of plants. The next stop was the compost pile.

They still bear fruit in old age; they are ever full of sap and green. Psalm 92:14

You never know what will happen to the seeds you throw around.

Our compost pile probably wouldn't measure up to a professional gardener's standards. As we cleared the back yard, we found a small hill--more of a lump really. It looked like, in a previous life, it might have been a compost pile, so we added to it. I throw all my plant-based kitchen garbage on it, and we throw on a layer of dead leaves from time to time. This spring, David ran the tiller over it a few times and then tilled some of it into the garden before I planted. Since it's not enclosed in any way, I'm used to finding stray weeds and grass growing up through the refuse. However, when I visited it last weekend, I was surprised by the two plants that were sprouting happily next to some discarded coffee grounds and celery trimmings. One looked like some kind of squash plant, and the other was either a watermelon or a cantaloupe plant. I'm still too much of a city girl to know for sure until they get a little further along. As I thought about that little accidental garden, I wondered how often some random act of kindness or an almost careless word of encouragement bears fruit.

⁶ I planted, Apollos watered, but God gave the growth. ⁷ So neither he who plants nor he who waters is anything, but only God who gives the growth. 1 Corinthians 3:6-7

CHAPTER 26

Four More Lessons from My Garden – 7/13/14

A few weeks ago I wrote about some of the spiritual lessons I've learned while working in my garden. This week I thought I'd share some of the more secular things I've learned.

First, I've discovered that a smart phone is a necessity for the modern gardener, especially if she's a novice. Last year it came in handy when I was waiting for the seedlings to make their way into the sunlight. Since I had no idea what a baby okra plant or a new zucchini looked like, I often Googled a picture so I didn't accidentally pull up something I had planted instead of a weed. With a couple of growing seasons behind me, I can usually tell the good from the bad, but this Spring I found another gardening use for my phone.

Last year I lost most of my zucchini, squash, and cucumbers to something that started out as white spots on the leaves. I used some kind of oily spray that was supposed to control fungus, but it didn't help much. This year, when the same kind of spots began to appear, I whipped out my phone, snapped a picture, and emailed it to the County Agent. He immediately responded that my plants had dusty mildew, and he told me what to use to combat it as well as where I could find it. The treatment worked, at least long enough for several rounds of zucchini to mature. The mildew seems to be making a comeback, but David sprayed again Saturday, so I'm hopeful that there may be zucchini bread in our future.

I've also learned that green beans are the crop that keeps on giving. Our neighbor Dirk Schutter, the garlic king of Rains County, gave me some green beans during planting season. While David will eat anything, green beans aren't his favorite, so I only planted a dozen or so. I was thrilled when my first picking yielded enough for us to have some for dinner several nights with enough left over to fill a couple of quart-sized freezer bags. I took half the next picking to my aunt when she invited us for lunch, and I gave some of the next picking to another neighbor. I've sautéed, stir-fried, and used them in soup, and they're still growing. Many of the lower leaves have turned yellow and fallen off, and the grasshoppers have turned a lot of the remaining leaves into their own version of lace, but the plants continue to bloom and produce. It is my firm belief that we could eliminate world hunger if we sent these beans to famine-ravaged countries.

The third thing I've learned is that, if I can grow it, I can pickle it or use it to make relish. That may be a slight exaggeration, but not by much. Two summers ago I learned to pickle okra; and last year I turned cucumbers into bread and butter pickles, tomatoes and peppers into salsa, and extra onions and peppers into a sweet and spicy relish. This year, needing creative ways to use the zucchini from the mildew-free plants, I made zucchini relish and zucchini pickles. Last year I tried to pickle jalapenos, but the skins were tough and the insides were mushy. I'll probably try again this year, and if the green beans keep producing, I may try pickled green beans.

Finally, I found a new guessing game based on a garden-related activity. Friday night at a home group Bible study, I held up my discolored thumbs and asked if anyone knew what I had been doing. Guesses included painting or hammering with a bad aim. Then Betsy, after examining my hands more closely, started laughing. "Shelling purple-hull peas," she said. Betsy is a real country girl.

CHAPTER 27

Texas Dirt – 8/03/14

There's something special about Texas dirt. I have felt that way from my days of making mud pies in our back yard in West Texas to the last few years of learning to coax a passable crop out of my little garden. This past weekend, I confirmed that belief in my own mind.

David and I just returned from Louisiana where we visited with his mom Betty. She fell a few weeks ago, suffering a broken arm and torn ligaments in her foot. Even with just those injuries, she would have needed some help, but combined with other health issues, she needed live-in help. She had been staying with her daughter Deb, but Deb and her family had planned a trip long before the accident, so we volunteered to fill in while they were gone.

It was easy to slip back into the caregiver role. It seemed natural to be sure she had nutritious meals and snacks as needed and to keep track of her various treatments and medications. I have to admit that the insulin injections didn't seem natural, but David, drawing on his experience as a Navy corpsman, was glad to take on that task. Betty's other daughter Sharon works full time, but she stopped by at lunch or on her way home to help her mom with grooming and other personal needs.

By dividing the caregiving among the three of us, none of us was over-burdened - but I still began to feel the familiar pressure that goes along with caring for a loved one. By the end of our two-week stay, I was in a state of emotional confusion. I was anxious to get back home to our simple routine, but at the same time, I wanted to stay and be sure everything continued to go smoothly for Betty. I kept these thoughts to myself, though, as Deb returned and David and I traded our caregiver hats for simple visitor caps.

The morning we left, we packed up the car, gave last minute hugs, and headed for home. I felt like I used to feel when I left Mom and Dad with my brother or a temporary caregiver for a few days, or later, the way I felt when I left for home after visiting them in their residential care facility. I felt the relief of leaving the responsibilities behind mixed with the feeling that I was somehow shirking my duties. I knew that we had done a good job and that Betty was in good hands, but my heart hadn't quite gotten the message yet. However, time and distance can be soothing, and by the time we crossed the Texas border, I was looking forward instead of backward.

We had seen reports of rain in the Emory area while we were gone, and I wondered if my garden had survived two weeks of neglect. As we pulled into the driveway, I was disappointed that I didn't see any red tomatoes shining through the protective fence we had built to keep the squirrels out. When the car came to a stop, I immediately went to check it out. I was relieved to see that the perimeter hadn't been breached and that there were lots of tomatoes just beginning to turn. I also saw some cucumbers and purple hull peas that needed to be picked and an eggplant that needed to be staked up.

I helped David unload the car, and then I changed into my grubby shoes, grabbed a small plastic tub, and went back to the garden. I only meant to stay for a few minutes, but an hour or so later, I had a tub full of veggies and dirt up to my elbows. I went back into the house to fix dinner, and as I scrubbed the dirt out from under my nails, I realized that the tension I had been feeling since we left home two weeks ago was gone. There really is something healing about digging in the dirt, especially if that dirt is in your own back yard.

CHAPTER 28

Faith, Garlic, and Gophers – 10/19/14

I'm moving a little more slowly than normal today. Yesterday, after a month or so off, I was back in the garden. Dirk Schutter, my neighbor and the garlic king of Shady Grove, has been spurring all his gardener friends into action by passing out bulbs and reminding us that October is the time to plant garlic.

If you've followed my column for a while, you know that I have a running battle with the gophers in my yard over my garlic crop. Two years ago, I started with twenty plants, and I lost a quarter of them to the little critter. Last year, I think he invited all his relatives to move in with him. I planted fifty bulbs and lost over half of them. This year, Dirk wanted to be sure there would be plenty of the tasty treat for both my cooking needs and for the snacking pleasure of my resident rodents. He gave me a large ice cream bucket full of planting bulbs.

Last weekend, in an effort to help me with my gardening, David fired up the tiller, applied the recommended fertilizer, and prepared the soil. This weekend, I raked out any residual debris, shaped the rows, and planted about half the garlic along with some cold-weather greens. I have room left not only to plant the rest of the garlic but also to try some new things like beets and turnips. I know I'm behind, but the Texas A & M website says it might not be too late. I also know that I may be adding variety to the gopher's diet rather than to my own table – but I have faith.

The writer of the book of Hebrews says "faith is the assurance of things hoped for, the conviction of things not seen." It is faith that keeps us moving toward unseen goals, even when circumstances are less than promising. I guess it's also faith that keeps me planting garlic – again.

CHAPTER 29

Gardeners Learn to Adjust – 3/22/15

In the past few years, my garden has been a source of both life lessons and writing material. This year, however, the cold, wet weather that has called for school closings has also kept me out of my classroom. The call of the outdoors is strong, though, and last week, in spite of the still-squishy ground, I spent a little time outside where I managed to learn something about expectations and flexibility.

Last year, I started my garden a little late, and the yield from some of the early vegetables was underwhelming. Determined not to repeat that mistake, I took advantage of some nice weather in February to get a jump on the season. The garlic I planted in October was doing nicely, and in anticipation of spring planting, I had left extra space between bulbs. Armed with an array of garden tools and great expectations, I planted seeds – lots of them. When I was finished I stood back and imagined the beets, turnips, lettuce, broccoli, spinach, cabbage, and mustard greens that would soon be peeking up between the garlic.

Then, the snows came. Before the first arctic blast hit, some seedlings emerged, but most of them disappeared, victims of either the sub-freezing temperatures or the hungry critters that left tell-tale footprints between the rows. There were exceptions, though. A few hardy turnips and mustard greens and most of the spinach defied the weather and continued to grow.

Even after being coated with ice several times, they stayed green, waiting patiently for the few days of sunshine when they could grow a bit and put on a new leaf or two. During one of the warmer spells, I was able to harvest a few spinach leaves and a turnip. The turnip was undersized and split, but I decided to rescue it from the ants that were crawling all over it. I didn't end up using the turnip itself, but the leaves, along with the spinach, added some zest and color to a couple of salads.

After the last snow melted, I began to watch the garden a bit more closely, waiting for the surviving greens to mature. I didn't know what to expect from the turnips since this was my first time to plant them, but I watched for the spinach and greens to shoot up like they did last year. Instead, the spinach continued to hug the surface of the ground, and the greens bushed out, looking more like leaf lettuce than the tall, narrow plants I expected.

A few days ago, I risked getting my shoes muddy to do a garden check, and I was surprised at what I saw. One of the mustard green plants, the runt of the litter, had bolted and had a center stem full of little green buds. I looked a little closer and noticed that the lower leaves on all the plants were beginning to yellow from age, and the spinach leaves, while still mostly horizontal, were large and fully ready for harvest. A three-day rain event was predicted to begin within the hour, so I ran into the house, grabbed some plastic bags, and went to work. I brought in two full bags and an extra handful of produce before the rain began again.

While I was racing to beat the weather, I didn't have time to think deep thoughts, but later I was struck by the flexibility the plants showed in very negative circumstances. They were blanketed in snow and subjected to freezing temperatures, but still they found a way to survive. Instead of reaching up for sunshine that was hidden behind the clouds, they huddled down to take advantage of the warmth that was stored in the earth beneath them. They continued to grow – just in a new direction.

As for me, I was reminded that, just because what I see doesn't meet my expectations, I shouldn't stop looking. If I had waited until the warmer temperatures and sunny days brought the plants up to the expected height, I might have missed a really good harvest – and those greens were really tasty!

FAITH

CHAPTER 30

The Party's not Over – 1/16/13

The table decorations had disappeared, the signs that had been suspended over the buffet table with fishing line were gone and the Fellowship Hall was set up for Bible study class. The multitude of signs pointing toward restrooms, registration and coffee were gone, and the masculinity of the men's rooms had been restored, the artificial flower arrangements having been removed from the urinals. A vacuum was running somewhere, and several of the youth were wiping finger prints off the glass doors. Extra chairs were gone from the sanctuary, and the Communion table was set and ready for Sunday morning worship. David and I boarded the shuttle bus that would take us a few other tired volunteers to the remote parking at the Methodist church. It looked like the Redeeming the Time Ladies Conference hosted by Believers' Baptist Church on January 12th was over, but it wasn't.

I wrote in a recent blog that we were excited to watch God do His work, and we were not disappointed. One of my regular readers commented: *Look at all you've done in God's house, and I bet He loves a party.* She was right; God does love a party. He showed up at ours, and He showed off. In spite of early morning rains, we had around 240 in attendance including men and children. That's 80% of the number we planned for, and any experienced hostess knows that a two-thirds turnout is phenomenal. In addition, we had more than enough loving child care workers, the rain cleared and the predicted cold front didn't hit until 5:30 pm. The kids got to play outside part of the day, and I didn't hear any unhappiness coming from the nursery or children's rooms, even from the workers!

Our men were amazing, coordinating parking in three locations, standing in the rain to direct traffic and help ladies out of their cars, greeting each arrival and holding umbrellas over them as they walked to the building. Check-in was a little hectic, but the registration crew remained cheerful and flexible, shifting lines from window to window to keep things moving and setting up an impromptu coffee service to keep everyone happy. One creative worker used scissors and tape to put together a name tag for a guest who was upset because her preprinted tag couldn't be found. In spite of the weather and the crowd, we managed to get everyone in their seats in time to start right on schedule.

Food service was equally successful. They served muffins in the morning, wrap sandwiches and pizza at lunch and cookies in the afternoon. They even prepared meals for several guests with special dietary needs, and although we worried about running short (it's a southern thing), everyone had more than enough to eat. We planned extra long breaks to allow time for everyone to be served and use the restroom in our limited facilities, but everyone was so gracious and everything went so smoothly that we finished the day 45 minutes early.

The physical aspects of the day went like clockwork, but the spiritual part was even better. The tech team set the tone for the day with a selection of praise music and a PowerPoint presentation that played during check-in. The praise team led us in songs that inspired us to worship and helped us feel the presence of the Holy Spirit. By the time Edwina Patterson began to teach, we were prepared, and we were all blessed.

I didn't get to sit in on all the teaching, but I was blessed in other ways. I did my coordinator thing, checking in with our outstanding kitchen crew to see if they needed anything and making sure things were set up for the next break. They never needed anything and were always ready, but it was a blessing to see them working together with such joy.

I wiped up water around the restroom sinks, and I put fresh rolls of toilet paper in the stalls. It was a blessing to visit with the ladies who were taking a quick break and to hear their responses to tracts and treats and positive signs, the little things our restroom hostesses had done to make the time standing in line a little more pleasant.

I looked in on the kids, and I helped draw numbers for door prizes. It was a blessing to see more smiling faces and to be reminded of the generosity of the local businesses who donated merchandise to be given away.

One of my favorite jobs was picking up prayer requests that had been dropped in the basket and delivering them to the prayer room. It was a special blessing to quietly open the door and see one of our men with his head bowed over a pile of requests.

But blessings or not, as the day went on, and hurdle after hurdle was cleared, I began to droop.

"How are you doing," said one of my hard-working committee members, slipping her arm around me during the last break.

"I feel like I'm about to come apart," I said with unexpected tears filling my eyes. "I guess the adrenaline that's been holding me up is beginning to drain away."

"Oh, don't do that," she said, giving me another hug.

I found my aunt and cousin who were enjoying some cookies. I sat and talked with them for a few minutes and felt better. After all, one more teaching session and it would be over – almost. There will be a debriefing party for the volunteers so we can share our stories and praises with each other. And we need to develop an ad for next week's paper thanking all the businesses that donated goods and services. There are also thank you notes to write. But wait – there's more!

Before she began the last session, Edwina had a few announcements. Because of a lot of feedback, she and Pastor Jason had scheduled a 10-week Bible study beginning in mid-February. In addition, there would be a follow-up mini-conference in early May to see how we were applying what we had learned. I breathed a little easier when she smiled and added that it would be a bring-your-own-brown-bag-lunch event.

By the time we boarded the shuttle to go pick up our cars, I had two sheets filled with names of ladies who were interested in the Bible study, and visions of follow-up phone calls and e-mails, publicity and logistics were dancing in my head. The conference had been a gift of love that a lot of dedicated people presented to our little community and to God. In 1 Corinthians 13:8 the Apostle Paul said "Love never ends." Since there's more love, I guess there's more to do, and the party goes on.

CHAPTER 31

Christmas Came Early This Year – 12/19/13

No, I don't mean that gifts appeared under the tree before December 24 or 25 – depending on when Santa traditionally makes his visit to your house. It's just that yesterday, December 18, seemed to be particularly filled with Christmas-y things and feelings.

First, we had our Christmas lunch at the Senior Center. In honor of the occasion, I donned one of my two Christmas sweaters, one of my two pair of Christmas earrings, and one of my two pair of Christmas socks. That in itself made me feel very festive. There was lots of other holiday wear at the Center, along with smiling faces and happy chatter. There was a special table filled with desserts prepared for the occasion by various volunteers, and there was a small goodie bag for each of us – a pen and calendar provided by the restaurant that caters the meals, a candy cane and a few miniature chocolate bars, and a card signed by all the Center employees. It wasn't much, but it felt like Christmas joy.

When we got home from lunch our neighbors were in our driveway waiting for us. They had just returned from a week in Branson and wanted to thank us for watching their dog while they were gone. We visited for a few minutes, and they gave us a small peace lily in a red pot adorned with a few glittered curly twigs. They left us with hugs and holiday wishes, and it felt like Christmas love.

I went to the church at 4:00 pm for a rehearsal. The youth group is leading a carol and Communion service Sunday night, and I'm subbing for the regular pianist. Some of the kids were already there when I arrived, and there was lots of laughter and teenaged energy bouncing around the sanctuary. The guitarist arrived with a ukulele – a pinched nerve in her neck called for a lighter instrument than normal. I could tell her pain meds had kicked in when she started playing a blue grass version of "Away in a Manger." We struggled to stay focused and to sing and play songs that were too high or had difficult phrasing or unfamiliar words. It was chaotic, but through it all there was a sense of Christmas worship.

After practice was finished, the teens left to get ready for their ugly sweater party, and based on some of the pictures I've seen on Facebook, they did a fine job of getting ready. The quiet didn't last long. The younger kids began to arrive with signed permission slips and flashlights – it was caroling night. After Ms. Carla gave instructions for the evening and everybody chose a buddy, we loaded 41 kids and 10 adults onto the church bus and headed for the Katy Subdivision. We practiced our carols on the way, and sometimes the front half of the bus was even singing the same song as the back half.

When we arrived at our destination, the kids piled out, hurriedly found their buddies, and formed a ragged group in front of the first house. Ms. Carla pointed to one of the boys, and he ran up and knocked on the door. When a woman opened the door, we began a strangely tuneless version of "Joy to the World," and a smile appeared on her face. Her smile remained through "Rudolph the Red-Nosed Reindeer"- complete with all the extra phrases the kids like to add. We ended our presentation with "We Wish You a Merry

Christmas." Waving and shouting "Merry Christmas," we straggled on to the next house.

We repeated our performance at a dozen houses around the circle. Sometimes we sang "Jingle Bells" instead of "Rudolph," but we always sang with enthusiasm. And we were greeted with equal enthusiasm. Some people ran back into the house to bring family members to the door, some stepped out on the porch, and some sang along. Everyone smiled, some applauded, and one little boy danced as we sang. We got back to the church without losing anyone and were treated to cookies and hot chocolate. It was an evening of organized confusion, but watching the children bring happiness to others felt like Christmas hope.

It was quiet when David and I got home. I warmed up some soup, and then we settled down to check our e-mail and read. When I dozed off in my chair, David decided it was time for bed. As I lay there in that twilight between waking and sleeping, the memories of all the joy and love and worship and hope of the day floated in my mind, and it felt like Christmas peace.

May all the blessings of Christmas be yours both now and throughout the coming year.

CHAPTER 32

Scavenger Hunt – 21st Century Style – 3/28/14

David and I serve as volunteers in AWANA at Believers' Baptist. AWANA is a Bible-based program for children from four years old through the sixth grade. The children meet each Wednesday night and spend ninety minutes singing songs, listening to Bible stories, playing games, and learning Bible verses. Once a month we have a special event like Backward Night when everyone wore their clothes backward and the schedule for the evening was reversed or Campout Night when we made s'mores. This week we had a scavenger hunt.

The last time I went on a scavenger hunt, it involved going around town and knocking on doors to find items on a list. You can't really do that in ninety minutes with a bunch of four-year-olds in tow, so our hunt involved photos and was limited to the ten-acre campus of our church. The adults had been asked to bring cameras, but I was worried when we counted cameras and came up short. Silly me! As we prepared to divide the kids into teams, our leader called out, "Who has a smart phone?" About half the fifty kids in attendance held up their hands, including a lot of the first and second graders.

Once we were divided into groups, we were given a list of twenty-four photo ops. Number five on the list was simple - take a picture in a bathroom stall. Our all-girl team was a little dismayed when I herded them into the men's room, but the door had been propped open so I knew it was unoccupied. Some of the suggestions were a little more complex, like the one that said to make a human pyramid. It was simple enough to put the bigger kids on the bottom and the smaller ones on top, but a four-kid stack looks more like a square than a pyramid. The one we had to take under a pick-up truck was probably the most fun, even if it was just a little bit scary.

Our team finished in second place. We would have won except David and I couldn't keep up with the kids when we had to go to the far ends of the property to find the dumpster, the pond, and the church sign. Everybody finished a lot sooner than expected. The instructions said the winner would be the team that finished first or the team that finished the most photos when time was called. By the time all the teams had reported in, we had almost forty-five minutes to kill. So we did what all good twenty-first century babysitters do - we watched a video.

Our tech man went to a Christian website, pulled up an animated short about Elijah, and projected it onto the screen at the front of the sanctuary. The kids settled down to watch, and all was quiet for a few minutes. Then the video stalled, and the tell-tale buffering circle appeared in the middle of the picture. The audience groaned and probably would have thrown popcorn if it had been available. In a minute or so, the story continued, but the spell had been broken. Restless kids whispered, switched seats, and asked permission to go to the restroom or to get a drink of water. Before long, the video stopped again, and although it re-started in a few seconds, it continued to stop at increasingly shorter intervals. Finally, our AWANA leader came walking down the center aisle like an old-time theater usher looking for patrons who had sneaked in the back door.

"Okay," she said. "Who's on Wi-Fi? That's why we're having problems."

At least a dozen little screens went dark, and a dozen smart phones were slipped into pockets.

Some of our special event nights have not been what you would call a smashing success, but the scavenger hunt is one we'll probably repeat next year. I know David and I enjoyed it, even if it was a little more high-tech than the hunts of our youth.

CHAPTER 33

The Surprises & Promises of Spring – 4/05/14

Spring is my favorite time of year because it's so full of promise. Although it's been a little late this year, spring brings the promise of warmer weather. The warmth, in turn, brings the promise of new and renewed life as new seeds germinate and older plants wake up from their winter nap. Animal babies take their first wobbly steps in the sunshine, and gardeners begin to till and plant, claiming the promise of a good harvest.

In spite of the many springs I've experienced, I'm still surprised when its promises are fulfilled. I know the trees will get new leaves, at least those that haven't succumbed to the drought, but I'm always a little bit awed the first time I realize I can no longer see the neighbor's house across the creek because the trees are dressed in fresh spring greenery.

This year we got an extra surprise. David has cleared the brush and most of the deadwood all the way back to the edge of the creek, and we have dogwoods. The trees themselves are pretty scraggly, but they are in full bloom and are absolutely beautiful. My irises are budding, too - another surprise since I neglected them shamelessly after I broke my ankle last July. In addition, my day lilies have all come back, and they even brought some new offshoots with them.

    My vegetable garden hasn't yielded many surprises yet, but it still holds lots of promise. The garlic I planted in the fall looked a little frost bitten after the freezing rain last month, but after this week's rain, it has really perked up. Our resident gopher will be pleased about that and also with the fact that I planted enough that he can have his share and still leave plenty for us. My spinach is coming along nicely, but my onions look a little puny and nothing else has come up. I haven't planted my tomatoes yet - the squirrels with just have to wait a bit before they start stealing them. I'm looking forward to the promise of a good harvest, even if it turns out to be the harvest of my neighbors who are better gardeners than I am and who love to share.

    I've been doing a series of blog articles about the names of God. Saturday's post was about El Shaddai, the All-Sufficient One who keeps His promises even when they seem impossible. As we approach Resurrection Sunday in a couple of weeks, I've been thinking about how surprised the disciples were to find an empty tomb. They must have forgotten Jesus' promise of new life.

*   Jesus said to her, "I am the resurrection and the life. Whoever believes in me, though he die, yet shall he live, John 11:25*

CHAPTER 34

Church Ladies – 5/24/14

I have a friend who is the minister in a small town in West Texas. For some reason that I cannot fathom, he began practicing Bikram yoga several year ago. Why anyone would voluntarily go into a room heated to 105 degrees and twist themselves into knots for 90 minutes is beyond me, but he likes it so much that he went to California to take a nine-week teacher training course. After the first week during which he suffered from dehydration, extreme nausea, and what I imagine as a steady diet of tofu and bean sprouts, he posted the following comment on Facebook:

So LA is supposed to be chic or cool or whatever...but I tell the truth: I'd love to see a Southern church lady in a flowerdy (yes, flowerdy) dress holding a Tupperware container of fried chicken and deviled eggs about now.

I laughed, but I knew exactly what he meant. I grew up attending small-town Baptist churches where I was very familiar with church ladies, ladies who looked a little like Aunt Bea on The Andy Griffith Show. They wore longish, flowered dresses and sensible shoes, and their long hair was pulled up into a bun. Most important, they could COOK! They made yummy refreshments for Vacation Bible

School, and potluck dinners were to die for - literally if you were counting calories and cholesterol. They knew that "nothin' says lovin' like somethin' from the oven" long before Madison Avenue did, and when word got around that someone was sick or there was a death in the community, they headed for the kitchen.

A lot has changed in the last several decades. Everybody has several televisions, machines of all kinds orbit the earth, and electronic communication has made us all neighbors, but there are still church ladies. They look different now. Instead of floweredy dresses, they wear the latest fashions or jeans or sweats. Instead of sensible shoes they wear spike heels, sandals, or cross trainers. Instead of Tupperware, they use disposable containers. They can still cook, though, and they still know how to offer love and comfort and encouragement along with their food.

In 2003 my dad spent several weeks in the hospital with some kind of mysterious brain infection. It was a time of extra confusion and stress for all of us. I checked on Dad several times a day, Mom required extra care because of her anxiety, and my job didn't go away because of our crisis. My brother came from Arkansas to help, and the day he arrived, my neighbor put on her church lady hat. She was a stylish paralegal during the week and a jeans-and-boots Harley rider on the weekends, but she knew her way around a Crockpot. She arrived at dinnertime with pot roast, salad, and peach pie, and the effect was the same as if she had worn a flowerdy dress.

A couple of years ago, my cousin lost her husband. Before the service, family and close friends were invited to the church where a bunch of church ladies served lunch. There were lots of casseroles and homemade desserts - lots of comfort foods - but not a flowerdy dress or a pair of sensible shoes in sight. There were, however, lots of sympathetic smiles and warm hugs as we visited around the tables, sharing sweet memories.

We left the church in a long procession headed to a graveside service twenty-five miles away. After the last prayers were said and the flag was presented to the widow, we gathered at the community center where more ladies had prepared more food. I saw a few flowered shirts, but they were mostly paired with capris and sandals. I don't know if the ladies were from a church, but the effect was the same - more time to gather with loved ones while others took care of the details.

Since I am now retired, both from the business world and from caregiving, I have had many chances to be a church lady, to serve those in need. It's very rewarding to stand on the other side of the counter, offering smiles and words of comfort and encouragement along with the barbecue and sweet tea. The dress code in Emory is casual, a nice shirt with jeans or slacks along with comfortable, if not sensible, shoes. Whenever I assure a guest that there is plenty of fried chicken for a second helping, I think of my yoga friend and wonder if his church ladies really wear flowerdy dresses.

CHAPTER 35

Church Ladies: from the Other Side – 8/25/14

I almost missed this week's newspaper. We have been in Louisiana all week, and I have fallen way behind in my writing. Thankfully, I can write quickly once I receive a gentle reminder that a deadline is looming.

We made the four-hour drive to West Monroe in just over three hours last Sunday when we received a call that David's mother was in the hospital. Betty had suffered with various lung issues for several years, so when she contracted pneumonia, it was critical. The family gathered and stood vigil, at her bedside when we were allowed into the ICU, and in the waiting room or by the phone when visiting hours were over.

The phone rang a lot. Sometimes it was the doctor giving us an update, and sometimes it was a friend. I overheard my sister-in-law Debra talking to one friend who wanted to know what she could do to help.

"A casserole would be nice. David and Linda are staying at Mom's house, and since she's been staying with me for a while, her refrigerator and pantry are pretty bare."

That was all it took. By the time we pulled into the driveway a couple of hours later, the church ladies were arriving. We received not only a casserole, but also green beans, Jell-O, fruit and veggie trays, cakes, pies, breakfast food, and all types of paper products. In addition, another friend who had just heard the news arrived with fried chicken, potato salad, and baked beans.

The abundance, which at first had seemed like too much of a good thing, was greatly appreciated as the vigil continued through the week. Then, Thursday morning, shortly after midnight, Betty simply stopped breathing. The family gathered in Betty's living room over coffee, cake, and other leftovers to comfort each other and to discuss the next steps.

On Friday, we celebrated Betty's life with an afternoon memorial service. As we prepared to pay tribute to a life well lived, more church ladies arrived with more food. Relieved of the responsibility of seeing to the basic needs, we were free to begin the long process of saying good-bye.

I've written before about being a church lady, but this was one of my first experiences of being on the receiving end of their ministry. When my parents passed away, the funeral services were not held locally, so the family gathered in restaurants before or after the services. It was amazing to feel the love that came with the more personal offerings.

The phones are quieter now, and most of the condolence visits have been made - but there's still food in the refrigerator. Last night David and I sat in front of the TV with his aunt and his sister, listening to the football game with one ear, but mostly sharing memories and old photos. From time to time one of us would go to the kitchen and return with a brownie, a handful of grapes, or just one more piece of ham.

"I don't know why I'm still eating," said Aunt Jerry. "I'm not really hungry."

We all knew why we were eating, though - and so did the church ladies (and men). When a loved one dies, it leaves an emptiness in our hearts and lives. The food doesn't really fill it, but it reminds us of happier times. It also reminds us that in times of trouble, we are not alone. Those we love will always be there to offer a hug, a shoulder - and a casserole.

CHAPTER 36

Wishing You a Messy Christmas – 12/14/14

Two years ago, David and I spent Christmas with his family. One of the highlights of the trip was the Christmas Eve service. The service was beautiful with lights, carols, candles, happy people, and excited children, and it ended with Communion and the traditional candle-lighting ritual. Still, something was missing.

As we entered the building, I saw a table by the door to the sanctuary. The first thing I noticed was a basket of tiny cups the size and shape of the cups that hold coffee creamer in restaurants.

"What are these for?" I asked.

"Those are for Communion," said my mother-in-law. "That's your bread and wine."

"Okay," I said, taking one tentatively.

Once we were seated, I examined my little layered cup. On top was a Communion wafer covered by a thin sheet of plastic, and the cup contained a tiny swallow of wine. Both elements were easily accessible by pulling an easy open pull tab.

I love Communion - the time of meditation and of remembering the sacrifice represented by the bread and wine. I had taken Communion in several ways, and there was always a connection that added meaning. I had received Communion while kneeling at a rail where a minister offered words of blessing, I had dipped a bit of bread into a cup held by a pastor, and I had sat in a pew where we served one another. But I had never taken part in a self-serve Communion.

Serving Communion to a large crowd requires a lot of work, and the self-serve cups certainly simplified the process. In fact, it was over almost before the crackle of plastic and foil lids died away. Still, I missed the time of quiet reflection of the slower way, and I missed the connection.

When we had come in earlier, there were also white candles in plastic holders on the table. These were familiar, and I remembered the first time I had held one - it was surrounded by a paper collar designed to catch any dripping wax. These new holders served the same purpose, but like the Communion cups, they were new and designed for efficiency. My first time was in a small church pastored by my brother Jim. As the service closed, we formed a circle. Jim instructed us to share our light and our Christmas blessings, and then he lit the candle of the people next to him. As the flame traveled around the circle, I heard whispers of *Merry Christmas, God bless you, I love you.* It felt like a truly Holy Night. The candle lighting has become one of my favorite parts of Christmas, but on that new and improved Christmas Eve, something was missing.

The pastor began by lighting his candle and instructing us to share our light, but he didn't mention a Christmas blessing. Instead he added instructions to be sure the unlit candle tilted toward the lit candle. The light passed through the congregation, and the sanctuary was soon alight with the glow, but it felt like we were focusing more on the process than the meaning. After we sang "Silent Night," the pastor closed with prayer. Then, he asked us all to deposit our

Communion cups and burned candles in the receptacles at the exits to avoid leaving a mess for the maintenance staff. Maybe that was what was missing - the mess.

Life is messy. We are born through a messy process, and we die, if not in a physically messy way, at least in a messy tangle of bureaucratic red tape. We live from one messy situation to another, but the lives that are most significant are the ones that connect with others in a meaningful way, somehow sharing the messiness and learning to deal with it. When Jesus came to earth, He joined us in our messiness. He was born in a stable, surrounded by messy animals and shepherds. He ministered to messy people; touched disgusting lepers; restored sight with mud and spit; ate with sinners; talked with Samaritans; healed on the Sabbath; loved the unlovable.

I don't usually make resolutions, but since that night I have resolved to be a little messier. I try to take the time to connect with others, even when it isn't convenient. I try to share my light and my blessings, even when it means a few stains on the carpet. I try to start off each New Year by asking God to "bless this mess," and when I look back at the end of the year, I find that He has.

CHAPTER 37

The Promise Never Changes – 12/21/14

Christmas is a time of tradition. By definition, tradition is the transmission of customs from generation to generation, but as anyone who has raised children knows, each generation feels a need to put its own stamp on any custom passed on by the previous generation. As a result, while Christmas is a time of tradition, it is also a time of change. Here are a few of them.

In my lifetime, I've seen a lot of changes in the Christmas tree. First, the natural evergreen gave way to the flocked tree which was covered by some kind of fluffy concoction that mimicked the appearance of snow. Next came artificial trees. Thankfully, the aluminum ones that were spotlighted with a spinning color wheel were short-lived, but the first plastic ones weren't much better. They were made of a green material similar to what is used on the end of party toothpicks, and they shed needles almost as badly as the natural trees. Artificial trees have since evolved to the point that it's hard to tell them from the real thing except that you don't have to water them, and they don't begin to droop after a week or two. Having perfected the tree itself, manufacturers have moved to the next level by adding fiber-optic lighting that eliminates the tangled mess of lights that never all work at the same time.

Shopping has also changed a lot. When I was sixteen, I went to work at Woolworth's in the Big Town Mall. Most of the year, stores closed at 6:00 pm every day except Tuesday and Friday when they stayed open until 9:00 pm. During the Christmas shopping season that began after Thanksgiving, the stores stayed open until 9:00 pm every night. As competition increased, some of the larger stores began staying open until 10:00 or 11:00 the last few days before the big day, but most stores were closed by 6:00 pm on Christmas Eve. Christmas shopping budgets were smaller, too, and there were no advertisements for thirteen-month loans to fulfill the gift wishes of your loved ones.

Candy, cookies, and other treats are still a big part of Christmas, but even that tradition has changed a lot. When Mom made candy, she kept a cup of cold water by the stove and dropped a small bit of the hot mixture into the water to see if had reached the proper stage of readiness. If the spoonfuls of candy were dropped onto the waxed paper too soon, they formed shapeless puddles, and if the candy was cooked too long, it was grainy instead of creamy. Today, even the most old-fashioned cook uses a candy thermometer for this task, and the more modern cooks use modern ingredients that produce a perfect result with much less fuss. Regardless of the method, there are always enough sweet treats to inspire resolutions of diet and exercise in the coming year.

Besides tradition, Christmas is a time of promise. The promise of the tempting packages under the tree changes with the age of the recipient and the consumer trends of the times. Still, the central promise of Christmas never changes. It's an old promise - a promise as old as the Garden of Eden when God told the serpent that the seed of the woman would crush his head. The promise was repeated throughout Scripture, especially by Isaiah who prophesied that a child would be born, a son would be given. The fulfillment of the promise was announced by Matthew when he said that the child Isaiah had prophesied, the one who would be called Immanuel or God with us, had been born in Bethlehem. Finally, the promise was extended beyond the pages of the Bible when Jesus said that He would be with us to the end of the age. May the joy and peace of the Christmas promise be yours this week as you celebrate the traditions of Christmas.

CHAPTER 38

Post-Christmas Decisions – 1/03/15

Christmas involves a lot of decisions: which friends and relatives to visit or to invite, which family favorites to put on the menu, and which loved ones to put on the naughty list and which ones go on the other list. Now that the New Year is almost a week old, most of the visitors have gone home, most of the leftovers have been eaten or thrown out, and most of the gifts have been put away. Still, there are decisions to be made.

The good news for procrastinators like me is that some of those decisions can be postponed for a while. However, every time I sit down in my chair and see the jeans and knit top David gave me for Christmas, I'm reminded of one choice that I have to make pretty soon. The clothes in question owever, Howeverare folded and laying on my ottoman awaiting their fate - will they be returned for a larger size, or will I lose the few pounds that are making them a *little* tight?

It's not really a difficult decision. Several months ago when David and I started the Wheat Belly Diet, I lost a few pounds. An older pair of jeans that had been fitting about the same way the new ones fit now, slid right on. Unfortunately, I've found enough things to substitute for the wheat products I eliminated from our diet that the missing pounds have returned. Having shed the pounds once, though, I know I can do it again. The decision is, do I have the self control, or do I give in to a larger size.

Granted, this is not a monumental decision with long-lasting consequences - except as the extra pounds affect my health. Still, there are more significant post-Christmas decisions that each of us has to make. As we see in the Gospels, no one comes away from an encounter with the Christ child unchanged. The shepherds left the stable filled with awe that bubbled out as praise to God. The Magi changed their direction after encountering Jesus and went home a different way than they came. Herod made his decision to try and destroy what he perceived as a threat without investigating it for himself.

Later in His life, Jesus held what evangelicals might consider the first altar call during which He challenged His followers to make a decision. After a discussion about who others thought He was, Jesus made it personal. "Who do you say that I am?" Some post-Christmas decisions are as simple as returning or keeping a gift, but after celebrating the birth that has affected the world for over 2,000 years, each of us will decide who He is to us.

May the blessings of Christmas continue to be yours throughout the New Year.

CHAPTER 39

Valentine's Day - Not Just a Hallmark Holiday – 2/14/14

Valentine's Day has a church history dating back to the 5th century, but it became associated with romantic love during the middle ages. There are some people, especially husbands who usually end up in the doghouse for their lack of romance and people who spend the evening sharing a pint of Homemade Vanilla with their four-footed roommate, who are convinced that Valentine's Day was birthed by Hallmark and Russell Stover to sell more cards and candy. However, Believers' Baptist Church found a way to celebrate the holiday that kept husbands out of the doghouse and gave singles a place to share in the festivities – and my husband David found a way to be one of the stars of the event.

Believers' hosted a marriage conference last weekend. The planned event elicited a variety of responses. Some of the older couples felt like, after several decades of marriage, they pretty much knew what they were doing. A number of men, and a few women, refused to even consider attending, and others already had plans.

Still, over twenty couples, along with several singles including a few teens, showed up to hear Ryan Dalgliesh present four sessions on what a biblical marriage should look like. Ryan liberally sprinkled his Scriptural teaching with touching and humorous stories about himself, his family, and his friends. He has an easy-going style that put even the most timid attendees at ease.

The Saturday morning session ended shortly after noon, and everyone scattered to prepare for Date Night - the finale of the conference. Creative volunteers decorated tables with a variety of themes including a camo table, a couple of Texas tables, and several traditional Valentine tables. Brenda German headed a kitchen crew who cooked up a delicious Italian buffet and a luscious dessert table. As the diners began to gather, it was obvious that, while some had opted to keep it casual, some had really dressed to impress their Valentines. With two couples per table, conversation was lively during dinner.

Then, it was game time, and David became a star. Names had been put into a basket, and contestants were chosen by a random drawing. The first name for the first game was mine. Two other ladies were chosen, and our task was to make our husbands as beautiful as possible in two minutes. One table had been vacated by the people who were in charge of the games, so I appropriated the table cloth. Since I didn't know how to jerk the cloth out without sending everything flying, I moved the dishes to the side first. By the time I fashioned an off-the shoulder toga on my model, I didn't have much time left, so I quickly tied a napkin around his neck and shoved the flowers from a centerpiece into his hands just as the time expired.

Next, the men were instructed to take a turn around the room so everyone could get a good look at them before voting for their favorite. As they began their walk, someone shouted *Strut your stuff*, and David took them at their word. He went into a hip-swaying sashay that had everyone rolling on the floor by the time he finished. We won a movie-night gift basket.

It was a great weekend. We learned some things about what God, who invented marriage, intended it to be; we spent some quality time with friends and with each other; we had a great dinner; and we laughed – a lot. Still, I guess we're both a bit sentimental and traditional. When bedtime came, we each found a Valentine on our pillow.

CHAPTER 40

Granddaughters, Broken Hearts, and Good Friday – 3/29/15

My granddaughter Zoe spends more time thinking about spiritual matters then the typical six year old, but having a mother who is a minister and a father who is a Christian author has informed her theology at a young age. Three years ago, when asked what God looks like, she answered, *She has a big, beautiful face.* She also announced that *Jesus likes birthday parties,* and after a Good Friday service she said that her heart broke into two pieces for Jesus. I hated the thought of her feeling so sad, but the fact is that broken hearts are a part of life.

When I was a teenager, I thought my heart was broken when the young man of my dreams showed up at church with another girl on his arm. When a shopping cart hit my new car, and later when I lost my part-time job to a more experienced full-time worker, I thought I'd die of a broken heart. Then, as I grew in experience and maturity, I saw what real broken hearts look like, both in my own life and in the lives of others.

While we lived in Florida, I worked as a volunteer in the counseling ministry at my church. Most often, I counseled with caregivers and women who were struggling with relationship issues. Two women in particular stand out in my memory as examples of the truly broken hearted.

I'll call the first lady Jane. She was single and had devoted her life to caring for her mother. As her mother's life drew to a close, Jane's heart was filled with anger, bitterness, and pain. She felt as if life had passed her by while she cared for her mother, and she felt that others who should have helped her had left her to carry the burden alone. She also feared a life full of emptiness and lack of purpose after her mother left this life.

The second lady who I'll call Ann was the victim of a lifetime of abuse. She told stories that would probably be considered too far-fetched for reality TV, and just when I thought I'd heard it all, she shared another horror story. For months we cried and prayed together as we tried to find and repair the pieces of her broken heart.

Both Jane and Ann went through heart-breaking Good Friday experiences. They huddled, like the Disciples in a locked room on Saturday, fearful and anxious and hopeless. Then, Sunday came, and they experienced the power of new life. Like Mary in the Garden, they heard Jesus call their names. They knew He recognized them, that He knew their pain, and that He cared.

After experiencing His healing touch, Jane blossomed into a beautiful woman who shared her loving heart with everyone she met. Ann emerged from the suicidal wreck that she had been and became a source of love and light to those who knew her. The healing these women experienced didn't come from any earthly counseling or human wisdom. It was a result of the anointing Luke spoke about spoke about:

The Spirit of the Lord is upon Me [Jesus], because...He has sent Me to heal the brokenhearted. Luke 4:18 (NKJV)

After I heard about Zoe's Good Friday experience, I sent her a message, and it's also my Easter message to anyone whose heart is broken in two pieces: *Hold on, Sweetie. Sunday's coming.*

CHAPTER 41

Fat and Happy – 8/2/15

I just returned from four days at the F & H Goat Ranch, so named because of the fat and happy goats that populate the front pasture of the five-acre spread about twenty miles north of Kerrville. The owner, Julee White, retired from the Dallas rat race and social scene fifteen years ago so she could move closer to family and devote herself, in part, to making the dreams of her two nephews come true. When those dreams included goats for an FFA project, Aunt Julee provided both the goats and living space for them. I don't think the project was very successful, but the goats didn't mind. They stayed on at the ranch, invited some friends, and became – well – fat and happy.

The goats aren't the only happy animals on the ranch. Their sizeable pen is shared with two white miniature donkeys and a Jesus donkey that has markings on his back in the shape of a cross. Two cats and two dogs have unlimited access to the house through a pet door into the laundry room, and a dog "cousin" belonging to Julee's brother is a frequent guest – uninvited, but always welcome.

Feathered friends also find a warm reception at the F & H. I counted nine hummingbird feeders on the back wall of the house, and thirteen houses and feeders in trees in the back yard. There were more feeders on both sides of the house and in miscellaneous spots all over the property. I commented to Julee that her feed bill must be enormous, and she agreed.

I was one of ten human guests from around the country who came together for a study called "Chains or Christ." We were greeted with open arms as Julee opened her heart and her home, especially the kitchen. We were treated to delicious casseroles, salads, and homemade pastries for breakfast and dinner. The "light snacks" that were planned for lunch were spread out in the breakfast room – a sink-sized basket filled with a wide variety of granola bars, various other baskets and bowls filled with pretzels, trails mix, and nuts; fresh fruit; and more.

In addition to physical food, we were spiritually fed by Jodi Denning from New Mexico. She described her style of teaching as "offering a drink from a fire hose," and she wasn't exaggerating. The material covered during the long weekend was rapid fire and hard hitting, sometimes leaving us breathless but always ready for more.

All the participants are involved in some type of Christian ministry, and although many of us were strangers when we arrived, we quickly bonded as we worshipped, shared, laughed, and cried together. As I write this, I'm hoping I didn't gain any weight from Julee's hospitality, but I'm feeling fat and happy, regardless of what the scale says. I feel as if I received, as Luke says, "good measure, pressed down, shaken together, running over."

CHAPTER 42

The Church Kitchen – 8/9/15

The SISTAs group held its monthly meeting Sunday evening, and as frequently happens, the meeting took place in and around the church kitchen. SISTAs, or Sisters in Spirit and Truth Always, is the name of the women's ministry group at Believers' Baptist, and a lot of our ministry projects involve food in some way.

Several times a year, we gather to cook for emergencies. We prepare casseroles and freeze them so they are ready when someone needs a meal because of illness or other troubles. We also hold fund raisers to support holiday benevolence projects, and these usually involve food – a spaghetti dinner, a chili cook-off, or this year's new event, an ice cream freeze-off. We also host baby and wedding showers, wedding receptions, funeral luncheons, and various other food-related events.

SISTAs is not the only group that uses the church kitchen. A group of our men volunteers every year to serve breakfast to players in the RISD athletic program. Some participants in the Family Matters Bible Study bring take-out food on Wednesday night so they can fellowship together before class begins, and the Summer Wednesday Bible Study has a special food theme for each meeting. Of course, we can't leave out the church-wide potlucks when we all share food, fellowship, and our favorite recipes around the table.

With so many people using the kitchen, the cabinets and storage areas sometimes become really disorganized. Believers' recently hosted the monthly Hunt Baptist Association Executive Board meeting, and SISTAs was asked to cater the meal. The baseball-themed menu was fairly simple, and the evening was a great success, but the volunteers realized the kitchen was in need of some attention. Sunday evening seven of us spent an hour or so laughing and talking while we straightened and labeled drawers, shelves, and closets. Hopefully, our efforts will make future events easier and more efficient, but considering our busy fall schedule, I wonder how long it will be before the kitchen is a mess again.

Ours is not the only church kitchen that sees a lot of use. Almost every church I've ever been in has a large area that is equipped to prepare and serve food for their members. Regardless of how different we all are in background, life style, interests, and other ways, we all share a need to eat, and fulfilling this need together seems to draw us closer. Some potluck grinches think churches put too much emphasis on eating, but there is a lot of biblical and historical precedence for the practice. Like anything else, we can have too much of a good thing as Paul points out in his letter to the Corinthians when he admonishes those who apparently used the communal meals as an excuse for overindulgence. However, when done right, a Sunday potluck dinner can sound like this: *"And they devoted themselves to the apostles' teaching and the fellowship, to the breaking of bread and the prayers." Acts 2:42*

While the sanctuary is the heart of the church, the kitchen can be a service center where the lessons learned and the commitments made during worship can be put into practice. Friendships are formed, joys are shared, sorrows are healed, and communities are strengthened in the church kitchen.

CHAPTER 43

Advent is a Season of Hope – 11/29/15

Advent is the first season on the Christian Calendar, leading up to Christmas and including the four preceding Sundays. Advent began this past Sunday. The church I grew up in didn't follow the church calendar, so I didn't know about Advent until I married Christian's father and joined an Episcopal Church. That church included Advent candles in their Christmas decorations, but I still didn't know much about the significance. I knew there were four candles, one for each Sunday, and a center candle called the Christ Candle that was lit on Christmas Day. That was the extent of my understanding. Still, when I saw a pretty Advent wreath centerpiece while I was shopping for decorations, the wreath became one of our Christmas traditions.

We didn't have family devotions, so I placed the wreath in the center of the dining room table, and before we ate, Christian would light the appropriate candle or candles. At the end of the meal, since he had become obsessed with birthday candles on his birthday in October, he would sing Happy Birthday to Jesus and blow out the candles. He loved our little celebration, so we did it every night instead of just on Sunday. It wasn't exactly orthodox, but it worked for us.

I now know that the first Advent candle is called the Candle of Hope. Christmas is the celebration of the Incarnation, the fulfillment of hope, the realization of promises given throughout the Bible. Of course, to children, their Christmas hopes are not usually so lofty. Instead, they hope that Santa will visit and leave lots of toys and goodies behind. As a parent, it's fun to fulfill those hopes while surrounding the whole process with an air of mystery and fantasy. Unfortunately, we don't always think about the fallout when the truth is revealed.

Christian continued to believe longer than most children. First, he was an only child, so he had no older siblings who were eager to spoil the fun, and second, we were very good at creating a fantasy. One Christmas morning after all the gifts had been opened, he went outside to compare loot with the neighborhood kids. He came in a few minutes later, in tears because the other kids had said that his gifts came from his parents and not from a large jolly man in a red suit. He was crushed, both by our deception and by the loss of hope for future Christmases.

We fessed up and explained that, although there was not an actual person who flew around the world and delivered presents, there was a feeling of love and generosity that was especially strong at Christmas. We told him that we attribute a lot of the gift giving to Santa because it's fun to pretend, and it's also fun to make other people happy. We went on to tell him that, now that he was in on the secret, he could be Santa, too. He could sneak presents under the tree and into stockings on Christmas Eve just like we did. The light of hope rekindled in his eyes, and for a few years Christmas Eve was hectic as we all tried to be the last to bed so ours would be the last gifts under the tree.

In his teen years, Christian became disenchanted with the nouveau riche lifestyle we were living, particularly the excesses of Christmas. He lost interest in the elaborate decorations, the shopping, and the gifts. I think his hope was that the spirit of generosity would extend beyond our family to those who had less than we did, but while we put toys and canned goods in several collection boxes and picked a name off the angel tree, it wasn't enough for him.

Now that he is a father with children of his own, he has had to walk the tightrope between being a Grinch and giving in to the constant pressure to join the excess. He and his wife have two adorable children and have to contend with several sets of overindulgent grandparents, but they have still managed to foster a good measure of the true spirit of Christmas in their family. This week, he posted his six-year-old daughter's Christmas list. I'm sharing it exactly as she wrote it.

- A slepover with Ellie
- To buld a Snow Man
- To go ice scating
- To go slebding
- A candy cane
- To go to Colorado (Note: She was born in Colorado, and many friends and family live there)
- To give the Homelis some of my toys

Notes like that give me hope.

CHAPTER 44

Advent is a Season of Peace – 12/6/15

Last week I wrote about Advent, the season celebrated by the Christian church that includes the four Sundays preceding Christmas. On the first Sunday, the Candle of Hope is lit. The second Sunday is celebrated with the Candle of Peace.

Peace is sometimes difficult to find in the season leading up to the celebration of Christmas as we know it today. Our days are filled with too much – too much spending on too many gifts, too much decorating and too many parties, too much cooking and way too much eating. Still, some of the most peaceful moments of my life have occurred in the middle of the Christmas chaos.

When I was a child, our Christmas celebrations were simple. Dad was a hard-working man who worked two and three jobs to provide for his family. We had everything we needed, but there wasn't a lot left over for what he considered frivolity. We always had a small Christmas tree – not exactly a Charlie Brown tree, but nothing like the tree at Rockefeller Center either. It was a live tree, usually a

Scotch pine with a nicely rounded shape, but it was never so tall that Dad had to cut off the bottom so it didn't brush the ceiling.

The only decorations we had were for the tree, and those fit in one or two cardboard boxes that were limp from years of use. We had three or four strings of multi-colored lights with the large bulbs that were popular then, and about half the bulbs blinked randomly. Dad was responsible for testing the lights and replacing any burned-out bulbs before he casually wound the wires among the branches. Then my brother Jim and I placed several sets of multi-colored balls, some of which were so old that the paint was beginning to flake off. We finished by hanging icicles, the old-style strands of aluminum that tended to tangle and cling together, no matter how many times Mom pointed out clumps or bare spots.

We completed the look by arranging an old white sheet around the base of the tree to give the impression of snow. It sounds a little pitiful in comparison to some of the elaborate displays that are shared on Facebook now, but to me it was beautiful. The tree was in the window of the formal living room that was only used when we had company or on Christmas morning. Sometimes, while the family was gathered around the TV after dinner, I would slip into the living room where all the lights were off except for the tree. I would lie on the couch, surrounded by the natural pine fragrance, and watch the shadows the blinking lights cast on the ceiling. The peace I felt was amazing.

As I mentioned last week, by the time I had a child of my own, I had bought into the excesses of the modern Christmas, and the peace of those solitary moments with the blinking lights was rare. Sometimes, though, on Christmas night, after all the presents were open, the guests were gone, and the dishes were done, there were a few quiet moments to reflect on the love that was behind all of the celebration. The peace of those moments was sacred.

Peace is not simply the absence of conflict. The first Christmas didn't come to a peaceful world. Israel was oppressed by Rome and its tyrannical Jewish puppet kings. Mary and Joseph were dealing with the social stigma of what appeared to be an illegitimate pregnancy, and their healthcare plan and travel accommodations fell way short of ideal. Still, the angels announced the good news of peace on earth.

Last week I received a text from my son saying he and his family were flying to New Mexico because his wife's stepfather was dying. A couple of days later, she posted two beautiful pictures on Facebook with the caption "Peace on the Rio Grande." Even in the chaos of unexpected travel, impending death, and all the emotional turmoil that goes with it, she was able to find a quiet place of peace. It is my prayer for each of you that, during this Advent season, you will find the peace of the season.

These things I have spoken to you, that in me you might have peace. In the world you will have tribulation; but be of good cheer, I have overcome the world. John 16:33 NKJV

CHAPTER 45

Advent is a Season of Joy – 12/13/15

The third candle of the Advent Wreath is called the Candle of Joy. Much of the joy of the Christmas season is connected with children. There is nothing quite so joyful as the eyes of a child who has just caught a glimpse of the gifts under the tree on Christmas morning – nothing, that is, except the eyes of a parent or grandparent who is sharing Christmas with his or her child or grandchild for the first time. The joy of Christmas is multiplied many times when children come into the home.

Christian was a little over two months old when we took him to his first Christmas Eve service. He had no idea what was happening, but he was delighted with the twinkling lights and the flickering candles. He laughed and cooed when the choir began to sing, and his joy was contagious. A familiar experience seemed fresh and new when I looked at it through his eyes. Unfortunately, his father had to take him to the foyer where his enjoyment wouldn't disturb the other worshipers.

Three decades later, I experienced the joy of sharing a singing Christmas tree performance with my grandson. Mattias was only a few weeks old, and he slept in my arms for the entire program. Although he wasn't awake, he responded nonetheless. During the readings and dialogue, he became restless and whimpered in his sleep, but as soon as the music began again, he settled back into a peaceful and what I imagined was a joyful sleep.

Now Christian and his family live 1,500 miles away, and we don't have the joy of spending Christmas with them very often. Still, I share the excitement of friends who are preparing to spend the holiday with their grandchildren, and I share the joy of children at church as they learn the real reason for the joy of Christmas.

Wednesday night is caroling night at AWANA, the children's Bible study program we host at Believers' Baptist Church. One of the carols the children love best is "Joy to the World." I'm not sure they realize that the words of this song come from an announcement an angel made to a group of shepherds two thousand years ago. It was a message about a child who brought joy to us all.

And the angel said to them, "Fear not, for behold, I bring you good news of great joy that will be for all the people. For unto you is born this day in the city of David a Savior, who is Christ the Lord. Luke 2:10-11

May the hope, peace, and joy of the season be yours.

CHAPTER 46

Advent is a Season of Love – 12/20/15

The last three weeks, I've written about the season of Advent – more specifically about the meaning of the candles in the Advent wreath. The first three candles represent hope, peace, and joy. On the fourth Sunday of Advent, the Candle of Love is lit.

The word "love" is used a lot during the Christmas season. Sometimes it's used in a very self-serving way as various merchants try to convince buyers that the jewelry, cars, and other gifts they offer will demonstrate love much more completely than anything offered by other merchants. Other times we use the word love to describe the warm, fuzzy feeling that comes as we share treasured traditions and make wonderful new memories. There are also times when we experience the deep heart connection of genuine caring. Rarely, though, do we come anywhere close to the love represented by the fourth Advent candle.

However, my granddaughter Zoe came close a year or so ago. One afternoon, she came home with a collection envelope and the enthusiasm only a five-year-old can manage after a busy day at Kindergarten.

"Dad," she said, hitting up the softest touch first. "Can I have some money? I'm collecting for school."

"I don't know, Zoe," he replied, giving her his full attention. "What are you collecting for?"

"I'm not sure, but I know it's for sick kids. Please, Dad. They really need it!"

He checked the envelope and saw it was a legitimate charity supporting leukemia research. Besides, she has had him wrapped around her little finger since before she was born, so he gave her his change and threw in a couple of dollars for good measure.

"Thank you, Daddy," she beamed, giving him a big hug before she skipped off on her errand of mercy. Before the day was over, she had approached her mother, her brother, and probably a few neighbors. When Christian went in to tell her goodnight, she was still excited. "Dad, I wonder how much money I collected."

"I don't know, Zoe-Zoe, but I'll bet it's a lot. I'll count it with you before you go to school tomorrow."

The next morning, she bounced in to the kitchen with her bulging, jingling bag. "Dad, can we count the money now?"

Christian's never been much of a morning person, but he looked into those big eyes and smiled. "Okay, but then you have to eat your breakfast."

He emptied the money onto the table, but by the time he finished counting, his smile had turned to a look of astonishment. "Zoe, where did you get all this money?"

"Well," she said, "I got some from you and Mom and brother and some other people."

"But there's over $50 here," he said, wondering if he was raising a little con artist.

"Oh, I also put some in from my piggy bank."

"How much?"

"All of it."

"Zoe, it took you a long time to save up that money."

"But, Dad, the kids really need it – and I can get more. Can I have pancakes for breakfast?"

Later, when he told me the story, he was still shaking his head in wonder. "Mom, I was feeling pretty self-righteous because I emptied my pockets, but she gave two or three months of her allowance and chore money without a second thought."

Zoe's story isn't a Christmas story, or at least it didn't happen in December, but hers is the kind of love the Apostle John wrote about when he said "For God so loved the world" and the love Jesus commanded when he said "Love your neighbor as you love yourself." During this last week of Advent, may you love and be loved with the abandon of a five-year-old girl who emptied her piggy bank. As we celebrate the birth of our Savior during this season of love, I think about what He gave up, and I wonder if He said, "Dad, they really need it."

Merry Christmas!

FAMILY AND FRIENDS

CHAPTER 47

The Nature of Generosity – 6/12/12

We've been the recipient of several generous gifts in the last couple of weeks. What makes people so generous with some things and not with others? Is it in the nature of the giver or the nature of the gift?

There's an old joke that asks *Why do people in small, quiet towns still have to lock their car doors? So no one will put a zucchini in it.* I was reminded of how bountifully zucchini produces and how generous people can be when our door bell rang last week. It was our neighbor who had just returned from a three-week vacation.

"My zucchini went a little crazy while I was gone," he said. "I brought you a couple."

Two zucchinis may not sound like a lot, but these were MONSTER zucchini. They extended through five meals and might have lasted another night or two except my zucchini fritters weren't very good.

The next gift started with an idea from a friend of mine. I'd give you her name, but she's a little shy. She wanted to make some sweet tomato relish and some sweet pickles.

"Have you ever made any?" she said.

"No, but I'd like to. Can I help?"

We set a date, and we set to work. We peeled and chopped and seeded and ground and made a big mess. I dripped tomato pulp on the floor and she used every pot in her kitchen and a couple from mine. We ended up with a gallon of sweet pickles and 10 pints of relish. Then we sat in the living room and gossiped while we listened for the jars to pop as they sealed. Even though she had paid for all the ingredients, she sent me home with pickles and relish and assurances that if we didn't like them, we'd adjust the recipes and make another batch.

A few days later my aunt who lives in Brashear invited us over for a visit and to "shop" in her garden. We came home with a shopping bag full of new potatoes, squash, zucchini (small ones), yellow squash, cucumbers, jalapenos, and onions. On the way home, we stopped by to visit our neighbor, and although we demurred on his offer of more zucchini, we took home several large bulbs of garlic.

There are lots of other examples of sharing all around us. Friends and family pitch in to cut and bail hay, or they water and pick when the gardener is out of town. Bowls and boxes of fresh produce appear on the counters at the Senior Center, available on a first-come, first-served basis. Excess eggs are brought to church to share with whoever needs them.

So, what is it that makes people so generous with some things and not with others? Do generous people intentionally plant more than they can use, or does receiving a bountiful harvest make people feel more generous? Does the perishable nature of the produce make people more willing to share what they can't use? If it wasn't so much work to preserve the excess, would people be less generous? If the way we handle our money is any example, it would seem so. We are certainly willing to store up our excess money "where moth and rust corrupts and where thieves break through and steal." I wonder if we would be more generous with our money if it was printed with an expiration date.

I don't have any answers, but I'm enjoying the generosity we've received. And in case you're wondering, my scrawny little garden is doing well. I discovered a tomato this morning. It's only the size of a marble, but it's a miracle nonetheless. If I get a good crop, I promise to share.

CHAPTER 48

Quality Family Time – 7/26/12

"The Family that prays together, stays together." The two sources I checked disagree about who actually came up with the slogan, but both agree that it was first used during the Roman Catholic Family Rosary Crusade, the post-World War II brainchild of Father Patrick Peyton. The slogan has been co-opted by others. In February of 1954 *Parents' Magazine* said "The Family that plays together, stays together," and in December of 2001, the *Times* said *"Those who cook together stay together. Maybe because they cannot decide who should get the blender."* My version would read "The family that spends time together, stays together." Not very catchy, I'll admit, but true nonetheless.

If you believe the ads you see on TV, quality family time consists of expensive vacations to theme parks or time spent playing video games or crowded onto the sofa watching the latest movie on demand while eating tasty snacks. I recently saw a version of quality family time that was quite different from the Madison Avenue version.

Believers' Baptist Church did another "outside the building" project last week at the Rains ISD Middle School. Some of us re-striped the parking lot while others scraped and painted the metal posts and framework of a patio cover. The volunteers included several men and women, two couples, and one family of four. The two little girls, ages three and eight, thought it was a great adventure. I thought it was a wonderful picture of four people who not only live in the same house and share the same last name but also live life together as a unit, a real family.

On the first day when we were doing prep work, both girls wielded scrapers, wire brushes, and rags and tested their balance, under the watchful eye of their parents, on ladders and scaffolding. The results weren't stellar, and the breaks for trips to the potty, snacks, and tending to boo-boos were frequent, but the sense of accomplishment and of being a contributing part of the group was beautiful.

On day two, the three-year-old tried her hand with a paint brush, and the eights-year-old did a great job with a roller on a long section of metal seating. Both girls added more paint smears to the same over-sized t-shirts they wore last year when we painted the school doors.

By day three, the novelty had worn off, and the girls and a friend who tagged along spent most of the morning playing. They squealed and giggled and did all the things little girls do when they're having a good time, but they also conducted themselves like children who are part of a family group and know what is expected of them. They ran back and forth between the project area and the athletic field where the football team was getting ready for the season, but they stayed on the grass and stopped to check for cars when they had to cross the driveway. When they got too hot, they went into the air-conditioned building and entertained themselves with toys brought by experienced and prepared parents, but they didn't run around creating havoc in the unoccupied classrooms.

The girls also got to share in the rewards that followed the work. We started early every morning before it got too hot, and as the mercury approached triple digits and the clock approached noon, we called it a day and went to Dairy Queen for lunch and ice cream. All of us, regardless of age, thought it was a fitting reward for being a contributing member of the group.

Years ago I worked with a lady who had a very different idea of family time. She was a single mom with a difficult job, and she relied heavily on day care. After work, instead of picking up her children immediately, she often went to the park for a walk or went home to take a quick nap. She ran errands, did housework, started dinner, and retrieved the kids from the day-care center just before closing time. When I asked her about it, she said that she needed some time to decompress after her day at work and that it was a lot easier to get her errands done alone. She also complained that her kids were demanding in the evenings and on weekends, always wanting to go somewhere or to be entertained, but that was all they knew. They spent the bulk of their time in a structured environment filled with planned activities and field trips and didn't know that family time was any different.

Yes, life is sometimes easier without the kids. They're often loud, messy, disruptive, and demanding. But Jesus didn't think children were a bother.

One day some parents brought their little children to Jesus so He could touch and bless them. But when the disciples saw this, they scolded the parents for bothering Him. Then Jesus called for the children and said to the disciples, *Let the children come to me. Don't stop them! For the Kingdom of God belongs to those who are like these children. Luke 18:15-16*

The family of four had to leave the painting project early on day one to take the youngest to the doctor for a check-up. As the mom herded her brood toward the truck, I told them all good-bye.

"You girls did a great job today," I said. They grinned and giggled their thanks. "I'm really glad you brought them," I said to the mom. "It's nice to see families doing things together."

"Well," she said with a Mona Lisa smile, "It's a family project."

I get the feeling that, in their home, life is a family project. If more people felt that way about their families, maybe we'd see more of the Kingdom of God right here on earth.

CHAPTER 49

The Schutters, Moving on Up – 5/21/13

David picked up his cell phone and dialed Dirk's number.

"Hey, I'm behind your house."

"What? I don't see you."

Dirk and Pat are our neighbors, but their back yard is fenced, and with the placement of their windows it would be hard to sneak past them.

"Well, I'm right behind your house. It's on the bridge."

I could almost hear the screams from the passenger's seat. We were on our way home from lunch at the Senior Center, and half of the Schutters' new house was in front of us, traveling very slowly down the narrow, tree-lined road. By the time we got within sight of their three-acre homestead, Pat, Dirk and their daughters Tracy and Rebecca had abandoned their lunch and were standing beside the road, cameras in hand.

When they first moved to Emory, Dirk built a cozy two-bedroom guest house with the intention of adding the house of Pat's dreams soon afterward. But other projects, especially those with Volunteer

Christian Builders and Campers on Mission, intervened and after ten years they were still living in the guest house. Then two months ago on an outing to Tyler they stopped in to look at manufactured homes "just for fun."

"I didn't really like any of the new ones," said Pat. "But the salesman said he had a repo out back. We walked in the door, and I knew it was exactly what I wanted."

For the next several weeks, neighbors watched in fascination as the Schutters prepared a place for the new house. A couple of trees bit the dust, several flower beds were moved and a lot of dirt was shifted around. A motorhome that had provided supplemental housing for guests over the years was winched out of the way. Dirk said the brakes were frozen in place after years of inactivity, but I think it was just getting back at him for dropping a tree on it.

Delivery day finally arrived, and David and I wanted to watch. The back half of the house was parked in the road just passed the Schutters' lot, and we pulled into the driveway, settling in for the show while the truck went back to the church parking lot to retrieve the front half of the house. A small crowd began to gather, partly because the only way to get past was through the ditch but mostly because this is the most excitement the neighborhood had seen since our ex-tenants left with their 50+ dogs. We pulled lawn chairs into the shade, sipped ice-cold water and speculated about how the delivery crew would manage such a huge task. One of Emory's finest even joined us for a while after he reassured a nervous neighbor that the house wouldn't cross anyone's property but the owners'. It gave a whole new meaning to the term neighborhood watch.

It was amazing to see the men maneuver the house into place with skill that comes only from lots of practice. They coaxed the two halves through turns that would have been tight for a regular vehicle, but seeing two 16'x76' structures pivot through a 180 degree turn and end up within inches of the intended site was mind-boggling.

The guys in the audience were particularly fascinated with the little tractor that pushed, pulled and lifted according to the remote commands from its operator. I think each of them was imagining how much fun he'd have if he could just get his hands on that joy stick for a few minutes.

That was a week ago. Since then various crews have come in to put finishing touches on Pat's dream home, and she and Dirk have started moving in some furniture. They had a family dinner there over the weekend, but I doubt they'll spend the night until the air conditioner is installed later this week. Regardless of how long you've waited, a dream house can turn into a nightmare in this Texas heat.

CHAPTER 50

Haute Cuisine or Country Cookin' – 5/2/14

Last week David and I were introduced to Poke Salat or Pokeweed when several bags of it appeared on the "share table" at the Senior Center. At this time of the year, people bring excess produce from their gardens to share with friends. The first time I remember hearing about Poke Salat was when Elvis sang "Poke Salat Annie," but the first time I saw it was last week.

The conversation that day was how to cook the "poisonous" weed to make it edible. I heard one lady say her mother boiled it seven times and poured off the water before she considered it safe. Everyone agreed that it was a tasty treat, but I wasn't sure if it was worth the risk, so I Googled it. I found that, while the purple berries and roots are toxic, if the leaves are young and don't have any tinges of purple, they are not toxic. I found a recipe that said to parboil once, pour off the water, and then finish by either boiling or frying. That sounded easy enough, so I took a small bagful home.

The thing about greens is that a small bagful cooks down to a very small serving, so I added some mustard greens from my garden. I washed, chopped, boiled, and drained. Then, I finished the process by boiling them in a little chicken broth with a liberal mixture of spices thrown in. David judged the results to be quite tasty, and neither of us suffered any ill effects.

This week, more greens appeared on the share table. There was a large box of turnip greens and another of tender greens - and there was a huge bag of poke salat. I didn't hesitate to get a larger bag of the poke, and at the encouragement of the gentleman who brought them, I added a generous portion of the tender greens. There was even more enthusiastic sharing of recipes than last week, and the consensus was that the best way to serve poke, after the requisite parboiling, was to fry it in some bacon grease and then scramble it with some eggs. That sounds an awful lot like spinach quiche which I love, so poke and eggs is on the menu for this weekend.

The comparison between the quiche and its country cousin reminded me of other similarities I've noticed between the Julia Childs and the Granny Hagan (my mother's mom) version of some of my favorite foods. I thought Quiche Lorraine sounded really exotic until I discovered it was bacon and eggs fancied up a bit. It took me a while to realize that sautéing was simply frying in a little oil at a low temperature, and that most sauces are fancy names for gravy. A roux is simply flour and oil, the base for every good Southern gravy, and espagnole sauce is brown gravy while béchamel sauce is white gravy. I guess if you say it in French, you can charge more, but a croque monsieur is still a fried ham and cheese sandwich.

Regardless of what you call it, though, people love food. We celebrate the joys of life with cake and other goodies, we gather as families and friends over shared meals, and we console one another with casseroles and covered dishes. Whether it's haute cuisine or country cooking, food draws us together like few other things do.

CHAPTER 51

On Motherhood, Co-Dependence, and Letting Go – 5/10/14

I loved being pregnant. For a co-dependent like me, it was the ultimate boundary-free relationship. I had an easy pregnancy, no morning sickness or fat ankles, but toward the end, he took up more than his share of space. Like a toddler who crawls in bed with you in the middle of the night, he stretched his 21 inches in all directions at once, wedging a hand under my ribs while standing on my kidneys and sitting on my bladder. I think God plans it that way so, by the time labor begins, you're completely ready to let go of the little bundle of joy you've been incubating for nine months. And that's what being a mother is all about – letting go.

It's ironic that a mother carries her child in her body for nine months, but unless she's a true earth-mother type who squats in the forest and gives birth alone, hers are not the first hands to hold her baby. Then, as soon as that blessed bundle is laid in her arms, there are other hands waiting to take him or her away - fathers, grandparents, cousins, friends - all eager to stake a claim on this new person.

The world at large makes its claim as well through baby sitters, church nurseries, day care, and playmates. A mother watches as her child adapts to each new situation, and she lets go a little at a time. One afternoon when Christian was three, a neighborhood six-year-old knocked on our door to stake his claim.

"Hi," he said. "Can Christian come to my house and play?"

My gut reaction was *No he cannot! He's just a baby, and I need to keep him right here under my watchful eye.* But I was raised by an over-protective mother who rarely let me out of her sight. It was a lonely existence, and I was determined to break that cycle with my own child.

"Okay," I said. "Be sure and hold his hand when you cross the alley."

I stood at the living room window and watched my little blond-haired boy, dressed in blue striped bibbed shorts, walking down the sidewalk away from me. Of course I cried. It hurts to let go, especially at first.

He's forty-two years old now, and I've had a lot of experience at letting go. Kindergarten wasn't too bad, because by then he'd been in pre-school for a couple of years. His first girlfriends were hard, because he always seemed to choose the ones that broke his heart. I guess that's not surprising, though, because I did the same thing until...well, until I met David. The hardest of all was the summer I released him into the care of psychiatric professionals for several months. I still second guess that decision, but through the experience he met the man he calls Doc who became a life-long friend and surrogate father, so some good came out of it.

For several years after his father and I divorced, there was a revolving door of releasing and returning. He went away to college but showed up on my doorstep most weekends. Regardless of where

I lived, I made sure I had a second bedroom, in case he needed a place to crash between semesters, and a garage big enough to store whatever wouldn't fit in his current domicile.

That ended when he took a job in Seattle. We had a couple of garage sales, and we called Good Will to pick up the leftovers. When the moving truck left, I had a real guest room and plenty of storage space, but as we said our tearful good-byes at the airport, I knew I was really letting go this time.

Then came the inevitable phone call.

"Mom, I met someone."

This one was different. Amy was the one for whom "a man leaves his father and mother and is united to his wife." He made it back to Texas for a couple of years while Amy finished her schooling, but then they went back to Colorado to plant a church. Now they're off to Portland for more adventures.

Thanks to phones and computers, I hear from him or about him daily. I sometimes share those daily updates with thousands of his fans and followers, but sometimes I get an e-mail or a phone call with a special message or question just for me. I'm still co-dependent, but I'm in recovery. I have a stronger sense of who I am now, and I've learned to set some healthy boundaries. There's still a special bond, though. I knew him first. I'm his mother.

CHAPTER 52

Family, Football, and Chili Cook-Offs – 10/27/14

I'm writing this late Sunday night or very early Monday morning according to the clock. It's been a long day, but a good one. If you've read the Believers' Baptist Church column, you know that we held our Third Annual Chili Cook-Off Sunday after the morning service. It was lots of fun, and it was a lot like the family reunions I attended as a child.

Planning for the event began several weeks - or even months - in advance. People who don't normally consider themselves cooks pulled out their recipe folders, and if they didn't have recipe folders of their own, they consulted Mom or Grandma or Uncle Joe who always made the best chili in the world. Discussions were heard in the hallways and the church parking lot about which cut of meat was best, which secret ingredient was sure to capture the taste buds of the judges, and of course, whether real chili should have beans or not. There was also a little bit of friendly trash talk going on, but it was all in fun.

Although chili was the main attraction, lots of other things were needed to round out the meal. The call went out for corn chips, cheese, crackers, chopped onions, hot dogs for the kids, tea, and lots of desserts. A shopping run was made to stock up on bowls, spoons, and napkins; and tables were set up in the Fellowship Hall to accommodate as many diners as possible.

David and I were among the first to arrive Sunday morning, but when we carried our contributions into the kitchen, there was already an air of excitement and anticipation along with the smell of simmering meat and spices. Smiles and hugs were exchanged, even between the fiercest of competitors, and there was love.

After a morning of worship that filled our spirits and a fun-filled lunch that filled our hearts and stomachs, David and I hurried home. We finished packing and headed east where we will be spending the week with his sisters in Louisiana, settling his mother's estate and making decisions about the earthly possessions she left behind when she passed away a couple of months ago. When we were halfway there, his sister sent us a text.

Instead of going straight to Mom's house, why don't you come here first. The Saints play at 7:30, and we're cooking hamburgers.

When we arrived, the crowd was much smaller - only six of us - but there was the smell of good food coming from the grill and the air of excitement that football stirs in diehard fans. There were lots of smile and lots of hugs, and there was love.

I didn't win either prize at the chili cook-off, but it was a really satisfying morning. The Saints won, but even if they hadn't, it would have been a satisfying evening. All day long there have been smiles and hugs and love. What more could a person ask for?

CHAPTER 53

Is There Birthday Cake In Heaven? – 11/2/14

Last Friday was the 86th anniversary of the birth of Betty Brendle, David's mother. Yes, she was born on Halloween, and I'm sure she heard every witch joke ever written and received lots of pumpkin-covered birthday cards during her lifetime. Her children swore that her love of sweeping had something to do with the connection between her birth date and brooms.

Betty passed away in August, but we thought of her on her special day. In fact, we thought about her a lot all week. David and I drove over to Louisiana last Sunday, and we spent the week with his sisters, going through the "stuff" that a person accumulates during eight decades of life. Betty was a very organized person, so there wasn't a lot of junk to deal with, but there are lots of memories.

It's a good thing we weren't on a tight schedule, because memories tend to slow things down. David and I spent several hours on several different days going through the tool shed and store room. Some items were packed quickly, but many became the focus of a story. *This was Granddaddy's hammer...Daddy and I built that gun rack when I was in the eighth grade.*

When the sisters arrived each day, progress slowed down even more. Each photo album or box of pictures evoked more memories and conversations about people I never met but who were a big part of the family history. There were tears and even a few sibling spats, but mostly there was a sweet sense of Betty's presence as we went through the grieving process together.

We didn't have a big celebration. David and I finished packing the trailer we rented to take home some of his memories, and the sisters had plans of their own as life goes on, but each of us remembered Betty on her birthday.

As I remembered, I wondered if there is birthday cake in Heaven. If so, that raised a host of other questions. Does each person get a personal cake, or is there one communal cake for all who share the same birthday? Is a candle added for each earth year, or does the number remain static at the age at which the person died? Either way, that would be a lot of candles.

From there, my mind wandered off on a writer's tangent. I thought of all those twinkling birthday candles, and then I thought of the multitude of twinkling stars in the sky. What if, instead of lighting candles on a cake, God places a new star in Heaven for each birthday? I like that idea - a lot.

Happy Belated Birthday, Betty. I hope you are enjoying your 86th star.

He determines the number of the stars; he gives to all of them their names. Psalm 147:4

CHAPTER 54

The Part of the Story the Veterans Don't Tell – 11/9/14

I posted this story on my blog two years ago. In honor of Veterans' Day, I wanted to share it with my Rains County readers.

David spent ten years in the Navy, two tours of active duty and the rest in the Reserves. His experiences give him an instant kinship with other service men and women. It's amazing how many hours can be spent sharing stories and memories. They complain about the rigors of basic training while congratulating themselves on having survived it. They talk about who was where during which campaign and how close they were to each other, and they brag about who got in the most trouble while on leave. Sometimes they even talk about their combat experiences, but there are some parts of the stories they don't share.

David's first tour was spent as a corpsman on the USS Enterprise (CVN-65), and he loved it. He loved being at sea and seeing exotic ports. He loved presiding over sick bay, learning to discern between the slackers and those who were really sick. He especially loved the time when he was allowed to drive the huge carrier for a little while. Then came January 14, 1969. Wikipedia describes it this way:

"During the morning of 14 January 1969, while being escorted by the destroyers USS *Benjamin Stoddert* (DDG-22) and USS *Rogers* (DD-876), a MK-32 Zuni rocket loaded on a parked F-4 Phantom exploded due to ordnance cook off after being overheated by an aircraft start unit mounted to a tow tractor. The explosion set off fires and additional explosions across the flight deck. The fires were brought under control relatively quickly (when compared with previous carrier flight deck fires), but 27 lives were lost and an additional 314 men were injured. The fire destroyed 15 aircraft, and the resulting damage forced *Enterprise* to put in for repairs at Pearl Harbor Naval Shipyard, primarily to repair the flight deck's armored plating."

I've heard David's version of the story, how he responded to the sounding of General Quarters as he had been trained, rushing to his battle station in Repair 5 on the hangar deck, not knowing what was going on or what danger he was facing. I've heard how he spent those few minutes in the fumes and heat and vibrations on the deck below the explosions. I've heard how afterward, he helped with the wounded and the dead, how he field-dressed the head wound of a young man and sent him on a stretcher to sick bay where he later died. I've heard the facts, but until a couple of days ago I'd never felt what lies beneath.

Several years ago, David discovered a website dedicated to those who had served and are serving on the Enterprise. He also follows news stories about the Enterprise, and he found one of interest on CNN this week. The Enterprise is scheduled to be deactivated on December 1 of this year, and the CNN website carried a story called *On the front lines of history: USS Enterprise on its last deployment.* The article gave the history of the carrier and devoted a good bit of print to the explosion.

David decided to leave a comment and asked for some help in wording his remarks. Thinking like a writer, I threw out a couple of suggestions, and then I noticed that he was sitting still, his hands hovering over the keyboard. Tears began to trickle down his face, and a sob escaped between clenched teeth. I went over, sat on the arm of his chair, and put my arm around his shoulders. He took a deep breath and pushed the overwhelming emotions down into that place where they have stayed for over forty years. With his permission, I'm sharing the story he doesn't usually tell.

"I was a corpsman during the fire assigned to repair 5. Repair 5 was located on the hanger deck, starboard side aft if I remember correctly. I still remember how I felt experiencing the bombs exploding and not knowing what was happening topside. Even now as I think about the exploding bombs my heart starts racing and the adrenaline flows. I still remember many of those who lost their lives that day. I didn't know their names, because I met them for the first time as I placed their burned bodies into body bags. I'm sure I'll never forget those who gave their lives to keep the Enterprise afloat."

To David and all those who have stories they don't tell, thank you for serving.

CHAPTER 55

Music and Alzheimer's: The Memories of Music Live On – 2/22/15

Music played a big part in the marriage conference we attended last weekend. Before each session, Micah Mariano led us in a time of praise and worship interspersed with a few personal words of inspiration. One of the stories he told was about his mother who had passed away a few years ago. As she neared the end, pain and medications took away most of her ability to communicate. Right to the end, though, she responded to music.

His story struck a familiar chord, so to speak, since the same phenomenon is common with people who have Alzheimer's. Following is an article I wrote about the subject a couple of years ago.

In researching the connection between music and Alzheimer's patients, all sources agreed that music has power. The Alzheimer's Foundation of America states that "[music] can spark compelling outcomes even in the very late stages of the disease." It goes on to explain how music allows patients who are normally shut off from the world to connect with loved ones and to participate in enjoyable activities. Music is also a valuable tool in managing agitation and other behavioral issues.

Music was always important to Mom. As a child one of her greatest joys was playing guitar and singing in church and at family gatherings. In later years, social anxieties and physical infirmities made her give up some of her music, but she still enjoyed congregational singing and occasional family songfests.

While she was living with me in her latter years, we attended church regularly. The senior adult ministry had a monthly luncheon that included some sort of entertainment. Mom's favorite was the occasional hymn sing where the audience sang along. One afternoon as we sang a familiar song, our eyes met, and for a moment, her eyes cleared and she was there, as she had been before Alzheimer's. It didn't last long. As the clarity faded from her eyes, she continued to sing, but I couldn't make a sound past the lump in my throat.

Mom's needs eventually exceeded my caregiving abilities, and she and Dad moved into assisted living. By the time he died five months later, she was pretty inactive. She smiled at everyone and offered hugs, she walked to the dining room with assistance, and she ate with gusto, but that was the extent of her participation. When I visited, we spent a lot of time sitting together, holding hands. One day the TV was on a gospel music show. I began to sing along, and Mom joined in. Her words were garbled and incoherent except when she came to the word "Jesus." There was no connection between us like we had at the hymn sing, but every time Jesus' name came up in a song, she smiled and sang out clearly and with conviction.

Mom was generally a docile, cooperative patient, but in the last few months before she died, she developed a chronic skin disease involving blisters. Her blisters got infected, and she was hospitalized for several weeks. She became agitated, scratching at her bandages and pulling out multiple IVs. The nurses put her in protective mittens to stop further damage. Even so, her hands were restless and she frequently asked if we were ready to go. Still, she relaxed when my brother played his guitar. She clapped in rhythm to the lively tunes, and she lay quietly with her eyes closed, humming harmony, during the more mellow songs.

She never recovered completely from her illness. She was placed on hospice care and moved back to the assisted living facility. When she died a few months later, we received a sympathy card signed by the staff members who cared for her. One of the entries talked about her musical participation:

"I'll never forget dancing with her and listening to her hum to the songs at church. Her place is next to Jesus and we will remember her smile every day."

CHAPTER 56

A Very Special Graduate – and Grandpa's Nerd – 6/3/15

I first published this post three years ago, but I have revised and updated it in honor of Kyle's achievement.

Kyle Robinson graduated from high school a couple of weeks ago. Achieving that milestone is remarkable under the best of circumstances, but Kyle has not faced the best of circumstances in his life.

Kyle is my grand nephew, the grandson of my brother Jim. He was born on September 24, 1996 - a beautiful baby boy with big expressive eyes - and then the seizures began. For the next several years, the doctors examined and tested, trying to discover what synapses were misfiring or what signals were getting crossed in that little head. They finally agreed that Kyle had cerebral palsy and would spend his life trapped inside a body that refused to respond to his commands.

Kyle's family was determined that he would not be isolated, though, and they learned how to communicate with him. Kyle was Grandpa's boy from the beginning. When Kyle was two years old,

I spent Christmas in Arkansas with the Robinsons. One evening we were playing dominoes, and Kyle was sitting in Grandpa's lap. With a mischievous glint in his eyes, he stared at Jim until he got his attention.

"What do you want, Kyle?" Jim said.

Kyle grinned and cut his eyes over to the glass bowl on the end table by the couch. Jim followed his gaze and returned the grin.

"You don't want a piece of candy, do you?"

Of course he did, and he got it. Every child knows what an easy touch Grandpa is.

Through the years, Jim spent as much time with Kyle as possible. There were times when circumstances separated them by miles, but there was always a heart connection. Jim was never put off by the messiness of loving Kyle. He dressed him, bathed him, moved him from car to wheelchair to bed, and fed him - always with gentleness and caring, but also with a good deal of teasing.

"Hey, Kyle, are you keeping up back there?" he would ask when Kyle was riding in the backseat of his van.

"You don't want any of Mimi's chocolate cake, do you?" The answer was always a roll of the eyes and a definite nod. There's always room for dessert.

"You're such a nerd!" During one of my visits, Jim elaborated a little bit about the "nerd" thing.

"I asked him if I should stop calling him that, and he said *No. Nobody can call you that but me, though*," Jim said, shifting his attention to Kyle. "You're Grandpa's Nerd, aren't you?"

The sparkle in Kyle's eyes and the loving look toward Grandpa were all the answer that was needed.

Increases in technology have helped Kyle communicate even more effectively. He now has an eye-activated computer that "speaks" and frees him from some of the constraints of his disability. It's slower than speech, and he sometimes gets left behind in conversations, but when he has something to say, he knows how to make himself heard.

In school, Kyle had an aide who took him from class to class and took care of his needs during the day. He did well, and this was his senior year. He was so excited about it that he began sending notes to his Facebook friends in September inviting them to his graduation.

David and I didn't make it to the graduation, but on Memorial weekend, we made a quick trip to Conway for a party his Grandpa and Mimi hosted for him. He enjoyed being the center of attention, and he worked the room like a politician. He has a motorized wheel chair that he operates with his head, and he scoots around at will. I managed to get his attention for a few minutes.

"So, what's next, Kyle?" I asked. "Are you going on to college?"

"I'm try," he replied. His grammar isn't always perfect when he's in a hurry.

I don't know what's ahead for Kyle. His summer schedule includes physical and other types of therapy to help his body keep up with his mind. After that, he may choose to continue his education, or he may opt to go in a different direction. Whatever he decides to do, his family will be right there, cheering him on, and I'm betting Grandpa will be the head cheerleader.

CHAPTER 57

The Truck Stop Crawl – 8/16/15

One good thing about being a prolific blogger is that when a column is due and inspiration just won't come, the archives will usually yield an interesting story or two. I found myself in that situation Sunday night, so in honor of the summer travel season that is coming to an end, I thought I'd share this story about my days as a traveling caregiver:

Parenting is never easy, especially on the road. When the objects of said parenting are not cute little rug rats but rather sweet octogenarians with Alzheimer's, traveling can be even more challenging.

"I have to go NOW!" Dad said on a trip from Tampa to Dallas.

David obligingly took the nearest exit and pulled in to a truck stop. It wasn't one of the big, slick shiny ones, but hopefully it had an empty stall available.

"I don't need to go," said Mom.

"I know," I said. "But I do. Why don't you come with me?"

Of course, as soon as we entered the restroom, she began crossing her legs and hurrying to unzip her jeans. Thankfully, both stalls were empty, so I went into one while she went into the other.

Now, Mom was a little paranoid, and she never met a lock she didn't want to engage. Her stall had two, and I heard both of them click.

"I guess I did need to go," she said while I washed my hands. It took her a while to finish her business and get pulled up, zipped up and properly adjusted. Then the rattling began.

"I can't get it unlocked."

"There are two, Mom. Undo the one at the top."

"I can't turn it."

I heard the edge of panic creep into her voice, and I sighed as I looked at the dirty floor. At least there was enough space for me to fit under the door. As I crawled to her rescue, I reassured her.

"I'm coming, and next time we'll go into the handicapped stall together."

CHAPTER 58

A Common Bond of Brothers – 10/11/15

One of David's favorite things about the Internet is the connection he has been able to establish with several of his buddies from his Navy days. Some of them were shipmates for a year or so, but some of the original friendships were of a much shorter duration. Doug was a fellow AOCS student – Aviation Officer Candidate School for the uninformed like me. Since they have found each other again, he and David sometimes talk on the phone for what seems like hours, sharing memories and news from the years since school. Even though they never actually served together beyond the sixteen weeks of intense officer training, there is an amazing bond that has survived for over forty years.

I recently witnessed another example of the power of the military bond. Robert "Bob" Dewbre was born in May, Texas, in 1925. He was inducted into the Navy in the fall of 1943, the same year he married Norma Jean Bass. He never saw overseas duty, serving out his two years and five months in Kingsville and Corpus Christi,

Texas. Two years into his enlistment, he received orders to ship out, but the war ended the next day, so he remained stateside.

After his honorable discharge in February of 1946, Bob served as deputy sheriff in Baton Rouge. Later, he worked for Ethyl Corporation in Baton Rouge and Kelly Springfield Tires in Tyler. He also raised a family, David Dewbre of Athens and Peggy Chaney of Carrollton. Peggy and her husband James were our neighbors for several years, and both of them were featured several times in my first memoir.

In spite of all the other hats he wore, though, Bob never lost his identity as a military man – but now he's fighting another kind of battle. Several years ago, his health began to fail, both physically and mentally. Earlier this year, with Peggy's help, Bob and his bride of seventy-two years sold their home in East Texas and moved into a senior living complex near Peggy.

Like many Baby Boomers, Peggy became a family caregiver, able to watch her dad's declining health and his rapid descent into the grip of Alzheimer's and multi-infarct dementia but unable to do anything about it. His increasing care needs began to take a toll on his wife, and Peggy made the difficult decision to move him into a nursing facility. Private care was beyond Bob's budget, so a couple of weeks ago, Peggy moved him into the Clyde Cosper Texas State Veterans Home in Bonham, leaving Norma Jean in a smaller apartment in Carrollton.

Wife and daughter grieved over the move, worrying that it would increase Bob's confusion and lack of motivation. The staff at his new home reassured them that he would be fine, but they also requested that they stay away for seventy-two hours to give him time to adjust. Both women fretted and worried as they counted the minutes until the next visit, and then Peggy sent me this email:

Well, God continues to amaze me! Mom and I went to visit dad today and could not believe the change in him. He was talking up a storm (although repetitively so at times), completing sentences like he has not done in a long time and cracking jokes. We could not believe he was so communicative! I even asked the nurse if they were giving him something other than his usual meds because of his much improved behavior/attitude and they are not. She said it was likely due to all the men there and the fact they don't let him sit in his room looking at the four walls and watching TV all day long.

It seems that contact with other veterans had worked in a way that doctors and medications could not. I asked David what he thought was the cement behind this bond of military brothers that defies times, distance, and even plaque encrusted nerve tangles that take away the memories of a lifetime. Here's the general idea of what he said.

The connection comes from the camaraderie and common bond of shared situations and experiences – even when those involved didn't serve together. It's similar to playing a sport but much more intense. Both relationships involve watching each other's backs, but the military involves life and death situations.

As an outsider, it seems to me that putting your life on the line for something bigger than yourself requires a person to reach deep inside and find out what's there. Being in military service seems to define a person in a way nothing else does. Along with her email, Peggy sent me a picture of Bob, looking fit and happy, wearing a Navy cap, and saluting anyone who might see the portrait. The caption she attached said "You can't keep a Navy man down!"

WARNING SIGNS OF ALZHEIMER'S

CHAPTER 59

Part 1 of 10 – Memory Changes that Disrupt Daily Life – 10/17/13

Mom died from Alzheimer's disease on May 20, 2012. I received many expressions of sympathy, but one of the most meaningful was a letter from the Alzheimer's Association acknowledging a gift made in her honor. It arrived in September which is World Alzheimer's Month. The *Leader* featured an article the next week that listed several ways to observe the month. One way was to speak up about the disease. I'm no authority about causes, treatment, cure, research, numbers affected, or what's on the horizon in relation to this insidious disease, but I have fifteen years experience as an Alzheimer's caregiver. The back of the letter from the Alzheimer's Association was devoted to an article titled "10 Warning Signs of Alzheimer's Disease." I've combined some of my experience with the information from that article into a series about the signs and symptoms of the disease.

The first warning sign is "memory changes that disrupt daily life." If you sometimes forget names or appointments, but remember them later, you're probably experiencing typical age-related changes. Here's the real warning sign:

One of the most common signs of Alzheimer's, especially in the early stages, is forgetting recently learned information. Others include forgetting important dates or events; asking for the same information over and over; relying on memory aides (e.g., reminder notes or electronic devices) or family members for things they used to handle on their own.

The first symptom I noticed in Mom was what I called "the loop." She asked the same question or told the same story several times in a fifteen-minute conversation. She often forgot where we were going, and she always thought it was her birthday, regardless of whose big day we were celebrating. And remembering new information was next to impossible for her.

One of the most graphic examples of her inability to learn new tasks came with a phone call one Saturday morning.

"An alarm is going off at your parent's house," said an unidentified female voice. "I can't reach them by phone, and you're listed as the secondary contact."

"You must have the wrong number," I said. "My parents don't have an alarm system."

"Oh, yes. We installed their system yesterday."

"Oh, really! Can you hold a minute?"

I called Dad on my cell phone. When he picked up the phone, I heard an alarm blasting as he frantically explained how Mom had accidentally set it off. With a phone at each ear, I relayed instructions to him and restored silence. Obviously, I had some investigating to do.

Mom and Dad lived in a small house on a busy, well-lit corner within sight of the police station, but a salesman convinced them they needed a full alarm system. Within hours of installation, they had set it off several times, and going over the instructions only added to the confusion. When they lived with us, Mom got confused if I bought a different brand of milk, so you can imagine how she dealt with a key pad, a number code, and a panic button. I started making phone calls and eventually worked my way up to the owner of the company. After explaining the situation, as well as how interested the media is in companies that take advantage of the elderly, I convinced him to take out the system at no cost.

When Mom first started exhibiting symptoms many years ago, public awareness of Alzheimer's was in its infancy. When someone misplaced a set of car keys or forgot a name, they joked about having "Some-timers," and some people stopped drinking soft drinks from aluminum cans and cooking in aluminum cookware in hopes of avoiding the disease. We were as uneducated as anyone, but if we had known the difference between typical age-related changes and the first signs of Alzheimer's disease, we might not have waited several years before consulting a doctor.

There is not yet a cure for Alzheimer's, but early intervention and treatment can slow the disease and increase your loved one's quality of life. For more information about Alzheimer's disease and related dementias, contact the Alzheimer's Association at 800.272.3900 or www.alz.org.

CHAPTER 60

Part 2 of 10 – Challenges in Planning or Solving Problems – 10/24/13

Last week I began a series of posts about the warning signs of Alzheimer's based on an article by the Alzheimer's Association. The first warning sign was "memory changes that disrupt daily life," and the second is "challenges in planning or solving problems." The article went on to explain what kind of challenges might be involved:

Some people may experience changes in their ability to develop and follow a plan or work with numbers. They may have trouble following a familiar recipe or keeping track of monthly bills. They may have difficulty concentrating and take much longer to do things than they did before.

Some of you might be thinking *Oh no!! I left the pinch of salt out of the zucchini bread last week* or *I chased that $2 error around my checkbook for a week before I found it.* That's not the kind of challenges we're talking about. Those problems can be chalked up to normal aging or absent-mindedness. I saw some of the challenges to be concerned about in Mom not long after I recognized her "looping" manner of conversation.

Mom was always an excellent cook but a nervous hostess. Her social anxieties made her worry about everything from planning the menu all the way through the clearing of the table after her guests were stuffed to maximum capacity. She shouldn't have worried, because everything she made was delicious. But as Alzheimer's began to intrude into her kitchen, I began to notice lapses: her dump cake had spots of dry cake mix that had been missed by the butter; her pecan pie, which was usually to die for, stuck to the pan; her roast was dry and tough. Then she began having trouble getting the meal on the table at all. Many evenings, after seeing her confusion and frustration, I stepped in to apply the finishing touches and bring order to the chaos. Finally, it got to the point where she gave up altogether.

"We can have Christmas at my house if you'll do the cooking," she said more than once.

She used her arthritic hands as an excuse, but we both knew there was more to the challenge than twisted fingers.

Even though Dad was diagnosed with vascular dementia rather than Alzheimer's, he exhibited some of the warning signs, especially in the financial area. At one point in his life, Dad was the bookkeeper for a lumber company. I'm sure he did an excellent job, because he kept meticulous records of his own finances. He had a notebook in which he recorded every expense, and his bank statement was balanced to the penny the day it arrived. But as the plaque built up in his blood vessels, this began to change. When I dropped in on them at lunch time, I saw piles of unpaid bills, unbalanced statements, and unfiled paperwork on the coffee table. And when they moved in with me, I watched him stare blankly at a bank statement for an hour at a time before giving up and putting it down.

He didn't give up control of his finances as easily as Mom gave up control of her kitchen. I gradually assumed management of his checkbook, at first tactfully asking if he would like me to write a check for his signature or pay a bill for him. After a while, I stopped showing him the bills at all. Instead, I paid them on-line and entered the transaction into his checkbook. At first he asked questions, but eventually, he gave up the challenge and left it completely to me. We were one step further along in our journey into Alzheimer's and dementia.

For more information about Alzheimer's disease and related dementias, contact the Alzheimer's Association at 800.272.3900 or www.alz.org.

CHAPTER 61

Part 3 of 10 – Difficulty Completing Familiar Tasks at Home, at Work or at Leisure – 11/3/13

Have you ever needed help – probably from a ten-year-old – recording a television show or using your new microwave/convection oven? Have you ever made a wrong turn when trying to get somewhere you'd never been? If so, don't worry. That kind of difficulty is not a warning sign of Alzheimer's.

According to an article by the Alzheimer's Association on the 10 warnings signs of Alzheimer's, warning sign #3 involves more serious problems.

"People with Alzheimer's often find it hard to complete daily tasks. Sometimes, people may have trouble driving to a familiar location, managing a budget at work or remembering the rules of a favorite game."

Dad never owned a GPS, but he was always good with a map and could find his way anywhere. But after his dementia asserted itself, he began to have trouble navigating even the most familiar territory. A few months before we moved from Texas to Florida, he and Mom moved in with us, and even though he had lived within two miles of our house for twenty years, he couldn't find his way around town from there. Once, he wanted to go to the bank, but he couldn't find it, so he gave up and came home. And then there was the day he REALLY got lost. He left the house after lunch to take Mom to the beauty salon, and I didn't hear from him for nine hours. He had no cell phone, and I was frantic, wondering how long I should wait before calling the police.

When we got to Florida, he got his license way too easily for a man who had trouble walking, signing his name, and finding his identification. He and Mom were usually content to stay home until I was available to play chauffeur, but one day they had a burst of independence and decided to go out for a hamburger. After an hour of driving in circles through our subdivision, they returned home and ate the sandwiches I had prepared for them. Shortly after that, I confiscated his keys.

Mom gave up driving without objection when her neurologist told her that her deteriorating reflexes made it unsafe for her to drive. Her difficulty with completing familiar tasks showed up in her daily game of Solitaire. She read or heard somewhere that playing games was good mental exercise for the elderly, so she developed the habit of playing Solitaire for a while after lunch. As her Alzheimer's progressed, she developed her own unique set of rules. She moved cards from one stack to another in a random manner that apparently made sense to her, but she continued to enjoy herself for a while. But after we moved to Florida with a new set of routines, her cards stayed in the box, and if I suggested she play, she was totally confused.

For those of us who are getting older than we care to admit, it helps to know that the small mental lapses we're experiencing are typical age-related changes. On the other hand, while there is not yet a cure for Alzheimer's, early intervention and treatment can slow the disease and increase your loved one's quality of life.

For more information about Alzheimer's disease and related dementias, contact the Alzheimer's Association at 800.272.3900 or www.alz.org.

CHAPTER 62

Part 4 of 10 – Confusion with Time and Place – 11/9/13

If It's Tuesday, This Must Be Belgium is a movie released in the late 60s about a nine-country, eighteen-day bus trip from London to Rome. If you've ever been on one of those whirlwind tours, you know the disoriented feeling of waking up with no idea of where you are or what day it is. In fact, if you're retired and are no longer tied to a work schedule, you may experience that in your own home from time to time. You might worry that this is a sign of the big "A," but according to the Alzheimer's Association, if by the time you've washed your face and had your first cup of coffee, the fog has lifted, you have nothing to worry about. The confusion with time or place that may be a warning sign is described like this:

People with Alzheimer's can lose track of dates, seasons and the passage of time. They may have trouble understanding something if it is not happening immediately. Sometimes they may forget where they are or how they got there.

When Mom went to the "memory doctor," the doc asked her the day of the week, the date, the season, the city, county and state where she lived. To her it was always Spring, it was always September, and she never knew the day of the week or the year. She didn't know the city or county, but sometimes she said we were in Texas even though we were in Florida at the time.

Dad still had some of his wits about him, and he had the doctor's system figured out. He let Mom go first, and he listened closely when the doctor told her the correct answers. He remembered them long enough to make it through his examination sounding relatively normal, but his problems with time and place orientation showed up when we went on a seven-week, sixteen-state trip in our RV.

In spite of weeks of planning and countless explanations of our plans and itinerary, Dad didn't get it. He and Mom rode in the "living room" of our forty-foot motor home, safely belted in on the sofa that made out into their bed when we stopped for the night. They commented on the passing scenery, and he sometimes followed our progress on a map, but when we stopped for the night, he was often confused. One evening we camped in a state park in Texas, and the three of us set up our chairs under a tree overlooking the lake while David took a shower.

"Where's my car?" he said.

"It's back in the driveway in Florida," I said.

"Then how did we get here?"

"In that big bus behind us."

"Who drove it?"

"David."

"Oh, is he here?"

"Yes, he's taking a shower."

He contemplated that for a bit, then said, "How's Mattias?"

Don't ask a woman about her grandson unless you want a five-minute dissertation. After mine, he said, "Do they have any plans to come see us any time soon?"

"No, but we're going up there when we leave here."

"Oh yeah," he said. "I forgot."

There was a lot of that going around.

If you or your loved one is more than a little confused about time and place, talk to your doctor. For more information about Alzheimer's disease and related dementias, contact the Alzheimer's Association at 800.272.3900 or www.alz.org.

CHAPTER 63

Part 5 of 10 - Trouble Understanding Visual Images and Spatial Relationships – 11/13/13

The fifth warning sign of Alzheimer's may be a little harder to observe than some of the other signs. Sometimes the evidence that someone is having trouble understanding visual images and spatial relationships is not as obvious as forgetting the name of a family member or thinking the year is 1985. The Alzheimer's Association defines this warning sign as follows:

For some people, having vision problems is a sign of Alzheimer's. They may have difficulty reading, judging distance and determining color or contrast. In terms of perception, they may pass a mirror and think someone else is in the room. They may not realize they are the person in the mirror.

When Mom visited the neurologist, he had several ways of measuring this type of understanding, but one of the most visual was asking her to reproduce a diagram of two interlocking squares. Needless to say, she didn't do very well on this challenge.

Before Alzheimer's, Mom loved to read. Between my 2nd and 3rd grade years, before she took a job outside the home, my brother Jim, Mom and I walked to the library once a week to load up on books to carry us through the hot Texas summer. While she worked, she didn't read much. She was too tired when she got home to do anything but eat dinner and get ready for the next day. But after she retired, the library once again became one of her favorite "go to" places. By the time she and Dad moved in with me, choosing a book to check out was becoming a difficult decision, but she loved the books I chose for her. She read a lot, and she read so quickly that I had trouble keeping up with the demand. But after a year or so, she slowed down a bit. I noticed that she had several books on her coffee table, all with envelopes, bits of paper, or paper clips marking her place. She picked up books at random and began reading, sometimes at the marked spot, but often on a random page earlier or later in the book. Instead of asking for more books long before the due dates, more often than not the books remained unfinished.

"Mom, do you want me to re-check these so you can finish them?"

"No, that's okay. Go ahead and return them."

Eventually, the books stayed on the table for three weeks, untouched, while Mom stared at quiz shows and Dr. Phil or dozed on the couch with Dad.

She also developed problems with perception when she was walking. At home, she stopped when she came to a doorway where the flooring changed from carpet to tile. After checking it out closely, she raised her foot high as if taking a step up or leaned forward slightly as if stepping down. She did the same thing when passing from areas of light to shadow. She also had trouble with the stripes in parking lots. I sometimes had to link arms with her and encourage her to step over what apparently appeared to her to be a ridge or a ditch.

These perceptual changes aren't to be confused with typical vision changes related to cataracts, and unfortunately there is no way to correct them. However, by understanding what might be going on, a caregiver is better equipped to deal with the erratic behavioral changes that come with them.

For more information about Alzheimer's disease and related dementias, contact the Alzheimer's Association at 800.272.3900 or www.alz.org.

CHAPTER 64

Part 6 of 10 – New Difficulties with Words when Speaking or Writing – 11/30/13

As a writer, I sometimes have trouble finding the right word for what I'm trying to say. Sometimes I refer to my Thesaurus, but I have to admit that sometimes I rewrite a sentence to use a word I can remember. I also have problems finding the correct word when I'm talking, but according to the Alzheimer's Association, that's a typical age-related change. If I start to have the following new problems with words in speaking or writing, then I have reason for concern:

People with Alzheimer's may have trouble following or joining a conversation. They may stop in the middle of a conversation and have no idea how to continue or they may repeat themselves. They may struggle with vocabulary, have problems finding the right word or call things by the wrong name (e.g., calling a "watch" a hand clock).

Dad didn't have this type of problem to any great extent. He was always a man of few words, and as he aged, he became a man of fewer words. In part, this was because he didn't hear very well. When I began taking a more active role in his health care, we had his hearing tested and had him fitted with hearing aids. Whether it was his dementia or his resistance to the idea that his hearing was deficient, the result was the same. He never learned to use his aids properly: he put them in incorrectly, he forgot to turn them on, he forgot to turn them off which ran down the batteries, or he forgot to put them on at all. After several months, I gave up the fight, and the hearing aids stayed in the drawer of his night stand. He seemed to hear the TV well enough, especially if he had control of the volume, and he seemed to hear Mom as they chatted on the sofa. But when it came to conversation with the family, he withdrew into his own little cone of silence.

Mom, on the other hand, became more chatty as her dementia progressed. Unfortunately, her ability to communicate what she was thinking didn't keep pace. She rarely used the wrong word; she just couldn't find a word at all. There were many times when she came to me with a light in her eyes, a woman on a mission, a woman with something on her mind. Then she opened her mouth, and after a few words, she hit a verbal wall. As she searched for the word that had escaped, the light faded from her eyes. If I suggested a word, it was usually wrong, and the fading light turned to frustration. Finally, the frustration turned to pain as she withdrew into the isolation imposed by the plaque tangles in her brain. I often offered a hug and words that I hoped would be comforting.

"It's okay, Mom. Go back with Dad and relax, and you can come back and tell me when you remember."

But she didn't. She didn't remember anyway. She came back often and tried again and again. As time went on, she tried less, but she still loved to communicate. When someone said something to her that she didn't understand or to which she couldn't respond, she smiled and giggled. But even to the end, she never lost the ability to communicate with a loving touch. To the end, she was always ready to open her arms to give and receive a hug.

For more information about Alzheimer's disease and related dementias, contact the Alzheimer's Association at 800.272.3900 or www.alz.org.

CHAPTER 65

Part 7 of 10 – Misplacing Things and Losing the Ability to Retrace Steps – 12/5/13

I spent most of my working life in the business world. I started in the file department of the First National Bank in Dallas and ended as an account rep for a company that designs and manufactures furniture and equipment for the salon and spa industry. I had titles that included, among others, stenographer, secretary, executive secretary, administrative assistant, and office manager. The bottom line was that people paid me a lot of money to keep them organized, to find what they needed when they needed it, and I was very good at what I did. When I got home, however, I wasn't always so organized. I've spent as much time as anyone searching for my lost keys, the misplaced remote control or the bill that's due tomorrow and was right here a minute ago. But when it comes to warning sign #7, misplacing things and losing the ability to retrace steps, no one could match Mom for originality and creativity. The official definition of this sign is:

A person with Alzheimer's disease may put things in unusual places. They may lose things and be unable to go back over their steps to find them again. Sometimes, they may accuse others of stealing. This may occur more frequently over time.

The first time I was aware of her penchant for putting things in unusual places, it was a windy day, and I was visiting Mom and Dad at lunch. Before I went back to work, I went into her dressing area to straighten my hair. I looked in the cabinet where she usually kept her hair spray but couldn't find it.

"Mom, are you out of hair spray."

"No, I'll get it for you."

She went into the bedroom, flipped up the edge of the comforter, reached in between the mattress and box springs and retrieved the missing can.

"Why do you keep it there?"

She looked at me as if I had a screw loose. "To keep it cool." Of course. Silly me!

That continued to be one of her favorite hiding places for things like her purse, empty prescription bottles and various lingerie items. Other places were the bottom of her underwear drawer and the back of her closet, sometimes on a hanger and sometimes on the floor under a pile of shoes.

She was also creative in the kitchen. Before she got too far gone to carry out the tasks, she helped with kitchen duties, including emptying the dishwasher and putting the dishes away. That always led to a game of "find the dishes" for me, but it made her feel useful. I learned to check food items immediately after she left the kitchen. Most misplacements, like the cereal in with the pots and pans, didn't cause a problem, but the ice cream in the vegetable drawer could have been really messy.

Shortly after Mom and Dad moved in with us, David and I were accused of petty theft more than once. Mom was convinced I had borrowed her sewing scissors and failed to return them, and one day I found Dad rooting through my dressing area looking for Mom's hair dryer. There was also a dust up of several days about the ownership of a vibrating heating pad, but patience and humor helped, and sanity of a sort was always restored.

While Mom thought we had some of her "stuff," Dad was convinced that David's clothes were mysteriously ending up in his closet. Every couple of weeks he came out of his room with a handful of hangers.

"I think these pants are yours, David."

"I don't think so, Elmer. I wear a 34/36 and those are 36/32."

"What about these shirts? I know these aren't mine."

"They must be, because they're not mine. They're mediums, and I haven't worn a medium for a decade or two."

Dad wrinkled his brow, still unconvinced, but he returned the unclaimed clothing to his closet until the next time.

If you have a loved one with creative storage practices, confiscate the important items like identification and insurance cards. Then sit back and enjoy the occasional game of hide and seek.

For more information about Alzheimer's disease and related dementias, contact the Alzheimer's Association at 800.272.3900 or www.alz.org.

CHAPTER 66

Part 8 of 10 – Changes in Judgment – 12/11/13

Have you ever made a bad decision? What about that used car that the guy assured you was in mint condition, or those expensive designer shoes that hurt your feet just a little bit, or that boyfriend you forgave because he swore she was just a friend. Yeah, we've all had lapses in judgment from time to time, but people with Alzheimer's take "decreased or poor judgment" to a whole new level:

People with Alzheimer's may experience changes in judgment or decision-making. For example, they may use poor judgment when dealing with money, giving large amounts to telemarketers. They may pay less attention to grooming or keeping themselves clean.

As far as I know, Mom and Dad only fell prey to scams a couple of times. The first happened before I realized there was a problem. Somehow they became convinced, either by themselves or by a slick salesman that they needed a living trust, even though they had no assets to speak of other than their house and car. By the time I learned that I was the secondary trustee, it was a done deal. When I took over management of their financial issues, I discovered that the trust had remained empty with none of their few assets being transferred into it. Thankfully the only loss was the $500 "legal fee" they paid to get it set up.

The other scam was the full-house alarm I wrote about in the first article in this series published in the October 22 edition. You remember: user confusion, accidental activations, phone call, blaring alarm, irate daughter, veiled threats, system removal. Less dramatic lapses in judgment resulted in missed payments and late fees that were easily remedied once I took control.

The part of this warning sign that was not as easily controlled was the part about personal hygiene. Dad especially became very lax about bathing and using deodorant several years before our Florida move. By the time we began to share living quarters, their cleanliness standards had slipped to the point that they became a major problem for a while. I knew this was a fairly universal problem for caregivers, because it was a frequent topic of conversation at our caregiver support group meetings, but I didn't realize how universal it was until I wrote a post for my blog called *Why Do Old People Smell Bad*. It became my most searched topic over the next few months.

The bottom line is this - don't beat yourself up about that car, those shoes or that boyfriend. Learn from your mistakes and move on. But if you or a loved one start sending the mortgage payment to your favorite televangelist, spending the food budget on the Home Shopping Network, or refusing to take a shower for weeks on end, you might want to consult your doctor. For more information about Alzheimer's disease and related dementias, contact the Alzheimer's Association at 800.272.3900 or www.alz.org.

CHAPTER 67

Part 9 of 10 - Withdrawal from Work or Social Activities – 1/05/14

We all sometimes leave an old hobby for a while to try something new, and we all sometimes get tired of work, family and social obligations. But someone with Alzheimer's may exhibit more extreme signs of withdrawal from social, family and work activities:

A person with Alzheimer's may start to remove themselves from hobbies, social activities, work projects or sports. They may have trouble keeping up with a favorite sports team or remembering how to complete a favorite hobby. They may also avoid being social because of the changes they have experienced.

Mom loved to sew, and she was very creative with a needle. She took pieces of favorite dress patterns and put them together in new and creative ways, and if she tired of an old blouse, she re-cut the neckline to give it a more up-to-date look. As her hands became twisted with arthritis and her mind became twisted with Alzheimer's, she gave up using her sewing machine in favor of hand work like adding or removing shoulder pads or replacing missing buttons and snaps. But even this eventually became too much for her.

While Mom was in the house sewing, Dad was usually tinkering with the car or working on some other guy kind of project. When he wasn't in the garage, he was working in the yard. As his dementia set in, he moved indoors and became a real couch potato, but he didn't become completely idle. He developed a love for crossword puzzles. He solved the daily puzzle in the newspaper and filled in the rest of the day with the puzzle books he received for Christmas, birthdays and other special occasions. He stayed with his puzzles longer than Mom stayed with some of her activities, but the incomplete daily puzzles began to pile up, and his puzzle books became a mess of erasures and crossed out answers. I caught him more than once filling in the answers by looking at the solutions in the back of the book.

Mom and Dad enjoyed their small hobbies, but neither of them played sports of any kind. They were spectators, though. Dad liked to watch the Rangers, and they both loved the Dallas Cowboys. As time went on, she lost interest in the football game and spent more time watching me or Dad than the TV, but Dad enjoyed watching football until they moved into assisted living.

Mom and Dad were never very social except with family members, so it was hard to see a lot of change in this area. Phone calls from them became less frequent, and they found more and more excuses for staying home from church. They rarely went out of the house and sometimes didn't go to the grocery store until the cupboard was completely bare. However, by the time they moved in with us, Mom had forgotten why she didn't like to socialize, and with David and me as "security blankets," they both began to enjoy attending church and going to church-related social events, especially if food was involved.

So once again the bottom line is a matter of degree. An occasional spell of boredom or a weekend of cocooning now and then is not a problem, but when this kind of behavior becomes a way of life, it may be time to consult an expert.

For more information about Alzheimer's disease and related dementias, contact the Alzheimer's Association at 800.272.3900 or www.alz.org.

CHAPTER 68

Part 10 of 10 - Changes in Mood and Personality – 1/28/14

The 10th and last warning sign of Alzheimer's is *changes in mood and personality*. All of us, especially as we get older, develop specific ways of doing things, and we sometimes become irritable when a routine is disrupted. Once again, Alzheimer's may cause people to carry this irritation to extremes:

The mood and personalities of people with Alzheimer's can change. They can become confused, suspicious, depressed, fearful or anxious. They may be easily upset at home, at work, with friends or in places where they are out of their comfort zone.

Dad's personality didn't change a whole lot with his dementia. He became a crabby, critical old man, but while he had always been a bit on the crabby side, he hid it better when he was younger and saner. People with dementia lose a lot of inhibitions, and although he was a man of few words, as his dementia progressed, he said whatever crossed his mind regardless of where he was or who might hear.

For example, he always seemed to notice when extra large people came into a restaurant where we were eating.

"She's fat!" Since he was hard of hearing, he wasn't very good at using his inside voice.

"Yes, Dad," I'd say quietly as I slid down in my seat. "She's fat, but she's probably not deaf."

His personality changes were embarrassing and annoying, but Mom's were extremely disconcerting at first. She had always been a little fearful, but she became the poster child for paranoia. She locked David out of the house when he went to pick her up for dinner one night, and she accused Dad of getting phone calls and having midnight trysts with a girl he hadn't seen in seventy-five years.

The neurologist concocted a medication regime that kept the worst of the delusions at bay – better living through modern chemistry as David would say – but she still had her moments. One afternoon I went to the grocery store and left David in charge. He was lying on the couch reading, and Mom and Dad didn't see him when they came out of their room and headed for the front of the house. They peered out the dining room windows at the empty spot on the driveway where their car usually sat, and David heard Mom start to complain.

"She's gone off in our car again. She should be here fixing us something to eat instead of out running around. She treats us just awful. She's probably out with some…MAN!!"

If Alzheimer's has a bright side, it's that sometimes bad things are forgotten. As Mom got worse, she forgot her fears and her accusations. Best of all, she forgot her social anxieties, and she became quite a party girl. She enjoyed going to church because she always got lots of hugs; she liked hugs even if she had no idea who was hugging her. And she loved parties. She especially loved party food, and other guests were more than happy to keep her plate full. Her sweet smile and her giggle made her a favorite, even when she couldn't remember the point of her story or the punch line of her joke. When she passed away, the people who cared for her in the last months of her life sent a card filled with personal notes. Many of them mentioned her ready smile and her sweet spirit. It felt like, in some small way, she had thumbed her nose at Alzheimer's in the end.

In the Association's article, there is an additional note at the end of this last warning sign: *Mood changes with age may also be a sign of some other condition. Consult a doctor if you are seeing any changes.*

Thanks for following me through this series as I spoke up for Alzheimer's. You may wonder why, since there is no cure, it's important to be aware of the signs of Alzheimer's. It's because early diagnosis gives you a chance to seek treatment and plan for your future. Your local Alzheimer's Association can help. Call them at 1-800-272-3900 or visit them at www.alz.org.

COMMUNITY

CHAPTER 69

Veterans Are Treated with Dignity in Emory, Texas – 11/13/13

History runs in cycles and so do attitudes toward veterans. When I was a kid, soldiers were respected, and even idolized, often portrayed as bigger-than-life characters on the silver screen. Then came the 60s and 70s, and young men returning from Vietnam were met with disrespect and even hostility. Instead of being welcomed home as heroes, they were spit on and villainized as warmongers and baby killers. More recently, especially after 9-11, attitudes have shifted back toward a more positive view of our military personnel.

But one thing that still seems to be lacking in the treatment of our veterans is dignity. In recent years, restaurants have used Veterans Day as an advertising ploy, competing to see who can offer the best special. Charities vie with one another to offer the most compassion to those who have been wounded or those who have lost loved ones in the defense of our country. Sometimes veterans are used as political pawns in heated campaigns. But there are still places where members of the military, past and present, are treated with dignity. Emory is one of those places.

This is the second year David and I have attended the annual Veterans Day Program at Rains High School. Once again I was amazed at the dignity displayed during this event. For those who were unable to attend, let me describe it for you.

The program was held in the high school gym. Various military vehicles were displayed outside the doors, boy scouts served as doormen, and teen-aged girls dressed in their Sunday best made sure everyone that came in was greeted with a bright smile and a friendly handshake. The gym was decorated with red, white, and blue bunting and a huge picture of a C-47, and one end was curtained off for the pre-program reception. There were favors including flag and service pins, mugs, and lanyards, and there was a beautiful brunch buffet.

After the reception, the friends and families of the veterans were seated on the gym floor. The high school students were seated in the bleachers on one side with the middle school on the other. As the program began, each of eighty-seven veterans was introduced by name, branch of service, rank, area of service, and commendations received and then escorted to his or her seat by a member of the Future Farmers of America. The introductions were followed by the posting of the colors by the high school color guard, the singing of the national anthem, the pledge of allegiance, musical tributes to each service branch, a ceremony remembering MIAs and POWs, and more. The theme of the program was "A Hero's Homecoming," and everything was aimed at making each veteran feel like a hero.

It worked. Smiles revealed the pleasure of being the center of so much positive attention, and tears showed the deep emotions behind the memories. Bent backs straightened as World War II and Korean veterans stood in honor of their branches of service, and flags were honored with familiar salutes.

The dignity and honor of the program was impressive, and the performance of the students who participated in the program was admirable, but what was even more impressive was the conduct of the students in the bleachers. They filed in with the expected noise of laughter and chatter, but as soon as the program started, a respectful silence fell. They stood with hands over their hearts during the anthem and the pledge, and they paid attention to what was going on, applauding enthusiastically in all the appropriate places.

There are many reasons David and I enjoy small town living, and on Veterans Day we experienced one more. In a time when dignity and respect are in short supply, it was refreshing to see so much of it displayed here in Emory.

CHAPTER 70

Thanksgiving in April – 4/13/14

I've heard of Christmas in July, but I had never heard of Thanksgiving in April until recently. If you've lived in Rains County for any length of time, you probably know about the Good Samaritans Ministry that offers food, clothing, and household goods to those in need. You're probably also aware that every year around Thanksgiving, local churches gather for a time of celebration and thanksgiving and also to raise funds to help cover the expenses of the ministry.

Last November, the annual service was canceled because of bad weather. Whether by design or because life gets in the way, the service wasn't rescheduled right away. Sunday night, five months after the original event was canceled, the Rains County Community-Wide Thanksgiving Service was held at Lake Fork Baptist Church.

Supporters of Good Samaritans, led by local pastors and community leaders, joined in a service that included a report of the number of families served, recognition of volunteers, congregational singing, special music, a challenging message, and an offering for the ministry. Afterward, there was a time of fellowship over coffee and cookies.

I heard a lot of good-natured joking about the unseasonal thanksgiving service, and I have to admit that I took part in some of it. As the evening went on, though, I kept thinking of the many times in the Bible when we were told to give thanks. As far as I know, there was no seasonal limitation put on those commands. In fact, Paul told the Christians at Thessalonica to "rejoice always, pray without ceasing, and give thanks in all circumstances," and he told the Ephesians to "give thanks always and for everything."

I'm thankful to live in a county that cares for those in our community who need a hand up. I'm thankful for people who care enough to donate time, money, and material goods to be sure that a hand up is available. I try to focus on being grateful, and as part of that attempt, I keep a gratitude journal in which I regularly write things for which I'm thankful. From now on, I think I'll make regular entries about the Good Samaritans Ministry, at least more often than once a year in November.

CHAPTER 71

Democracy in Emory – 3/14/15

When I sit down to write an article, I sometimes begin with definitions. This was one of those times. I found several definitions of democracy, but all of them began with government "by the people." That's a concept we take for granted and a phrase we throw around when we're feeling patriotic. What we often forget, though, is that a democracy is run, not by all the people but by the people who choose to participate. We saw a great example of democracy by the people in Emory recently.

At the February meeting of the Commissioners Court, a decision was made to hold the Founder's Day concert on the courthouse square. If that were all, the democratic process might have ended there, but the decision was also made to allow the sale and consumption of alcohol, and that's when the people spoke up.

As a writer, I not only produce words, but I read a lot of them, and there are usually a lot more of them than I have time for. I'm sometimes several weeks behind on even the most important reading like my son's blog and the latest *Leader*. Because of that, I wasn't aware of the decision until a couple of weeks ago at our weekly home group Bible study. The issue was brought up during share and prayer time by a member who was concerned.

After that, I began to hear a little more talk around town about the concert. I admit to being a bit of a cynic when it comes to politics. A lot of people talk about it, or post comments on Facebook, but too many people don't do anything about it. Then, Wednesday I received a call at the church office from a concerned citizen. She called my attention to the front page article in the *Leader*, which I had not yet read, and asked that I spread the word. Because the original agenda didn't specifically mention alcohol, the Commissioners Court was scheduled to revisit the issue at their meeting on Thursday. The caller asked that we pray and that we also consider attending the meeting - actually get involved.

Living up to my own cynicism, I breathed a quick prayer for wisdom for the court, posted the information on the church Facebook page, and moved on to other things. By the time I remembered it again on Thursday morning, I had missed the meeting. Fortunately, many other Emory residents were better examples of democracy at work than I am. They showed up at the meeting in force where one person spoke in favor of the proposal and two expressed their opposition to it. Whether it was the eloquence of the dissenters, or the many phone calls the court had received, the previous 3-1-1 vote for the proposal was reversed with a unanimous vote against it.

Since then, I've spoken to several people who bemoaned the loss of revenue this decision represents, and others who are thrilled with it. Regardless of which side of the fence you're on, though, it's encouraging to see that our little town has a firm grasp on how democracy - government by the people - is supposed to work.

CHAPTER 72

Community – 7/5/15

The most common definition of community is *a group of people living in the same place*. When David and I left our home group Bible study on Friday night, I turned to him and said, "Now that's what community is all about." While Emory is a wonderful place to live, I was referring to the kind of community that is defined as *a feeling of fellowship with others as a result of sharing common attitudes, interests, and goals*.

Our home group began meeting over a year ago, and we've been through a lot together. The obvious purpose of the group is to study the Bible. Darren Brumit, the Student Minister at Believers' Baptist Church, has led us through a ten-month study of the book of Hebrews, and now we're working our way through the Minor Prophets. As you might have guessed, speed is not a high priority. We ask lots of questions, and we don't move on until everyone is ready. Through the process, we learn a lot about God, and we learn a lot about each other.

The group is stable but not static. Attendance averages around twenty, but it's not always the same twenty. Sometimes Pastor Darren misses because he's helping Pastor Jason announce a Wildcat football game. One family misses occasionally because the mom is running a marathon, another because the kids have t-ball, and others because family is visiting from out of town. They always come back, though, or almost always. One family moved to be closer to work, and another couple relocated when he was called to serve a church as youth minister. Although we miss the ones who leave, new people and families join us, not filling the empty spaces, but creating their own places in the group.

Sometimes, especially when a meeting is near a holiday, we reluctantly cancel. We considered canceling last Friday, but enough of us were free that we decided to go ahead and get together. By Friday morning, only three people had signed up on the wiki page. Did I mention that we eat before we study? We take turns providing the main dish and then sign up for side dishes, dessert, and so forth. Last week, in addition to the light sign up, we had a couple of last minute cancellations, but food had already been prepared, so seven of us gathered around a huge brisket, a large twice-baked-potato casserole, and a punch bowl full of Death by Chocolate.

Pastor Darren was one of the cancellations, so we planned an evening of fellowship around the table followed by a game or two. Before we finished dessert, the hostess received a text from one family who has missed several weeks due to a very stressful summer schedule.

"We need a break. We're coming over."

"Tell them there's still plenty of food," I quipped. The reply was a happy face.

Before the tired family arrived, we received another message from the young couple who took on the youth ministry in another town. They were doing some odd jobs locally and were looking for a place to grab a quick bite before heading home to plan for an upcoming youth camp. There was plenty of food for two more.

The six latecomers arrived around the same time and were greeted with smiles and hugs before they grabbed a plate. Those of us who had finished eating moved to the couch to make room at the table. The conversation began with questions about work and then moved on to more pleasant topics as we filled in what we had missed in each other's lives. After everyone had eaten, we shared blessings and needs, and then we spent a few minutes in prayer. By the time we said "Amen," tense expressions were replaced by relaxed smiles, and a rousing game of Spoons ensued. Some played while some sat on that sidelines and cheered for their favorites, but all of us laughed and had a great time.

Our Friday night home group is diverse, with members who are still in college and members who are retired. Some members are waiting for the right time to start a family while others share pictures of their grandchildren. Still, in diversity there is unity - *a feeling of fellowship with others as a result of sharing common attitudes, interests, and goals.* That's community - that's family.

CHAPTER 73

Observations from the County Fair – 9/20/15

After living in Emory for almost five years, I finally made it to the Rains County Fair last week. It's not that I avoided it up to this point, but all my prior fair experience was with the Texas State Fair in Dallas. That one runs for two weeks plus an extra weekend, so there's time to dawdle over the decision about whether or not to go. The County Fair, though, lasts only five days, and in previous years, it was over before I hardly knew it had opened.

This year, however, I shared a booth with Kent Larson, another local Christian author, and I spent almost twenty hours at the Fair. I sold a few books, but mostly I chatted with people and learned more about life in small-town America. Here are some of my observations:

1. A parking pass is almost worth the price of the booth rental.
2. A booth beside the path to the restrooms is a mixed blessing. At some point during the evening, almost everyone will walk - or run - past you, but they are often too focused on their destination to stop.

3. A booth that offers a Christian memoir about caregiving, a Christian novel about baseball, and free pens has something of interest to almost everybody – with the exception mentioned in Observation #2.
4. Country girls look awesome when they're dressed to compete in a beauty pageant, but after it's over, they can hardly wait to get back into their jeans.
5. Country folks know what a trash can is for. Even on the last night there was almost no litter to be seen either outside or in the exhibit building.
6. I didn't see any salt water taffy, but other than that, the Rains County Fair was equal if not superior to the State Fair in junk food.
7. Rains County kids know how to have a good time without being disrespectful or destructive.
8. I have lots of very nice readers who took the time to stop by the booth to chat and ask about Kitty.
9. Mutton busting has to be the cutest event ever, especially the junior-sized rodeo clowns.
10. Asking your booth partner, who raises cattle, why some of the cows in the livestock area are so bony is a sure way to prove that you're still a city girl.

THE WHEAT BELLY DIET

CHAPTER 74

The Great Brendle Wheat Belly Experiment – 3/7/14

David and I both had our annual physicals last month, and it came as no surprise to either of us that both our doctors mentioned our weight. I've averaged an extra pound for each of the fourteen years of our marriage, and he's doubled that. Neither of us is what you'd call overweight, but we're both approaching our I'm-not-going-there limits. In addition, we both have blood chemistry issues. His cholesterol is high, my triglycerides are high, and both of us have low HDL levels.

I once spent some phone time with a wellness coach provided by my insurance company, and she told me the only way to raise my HDL level (the good cholesterol) was by exercise. I guess David's doctor agrees, because she told him to take a brisk walk every day. You can see how well that's going as I sit here at my keyboard and he sits on the couch with his second cup of coffee, reading a Terri Blackstock novel. In our defense, he plans to work on his tree cutting and burning later, and I have a date with the weeds in my garden.

As for his cholesterol and my triglycerides, those aren't new issues. I once attacked his problem by following a low cholesterol cookbook, but that was several years and several pounds ago. We've both gotten lazy since then. My doctor and I have tried attacking my problem chemically, first with fish oil and then with timed-release niacin, neither of which worked. At this visit, he said the only way to lower the level is to lose a few pounds. To his credit, he used his best bedside manner, looked at me, and said I didn't have a lot to lose. It was enough to keep me from stabbing him with a tongue depressor. Then he said he was reading a book called *Wheat Belly* and that I might want to take a look at it. Almost as if by divine intervention, the book appeared.

Well, not exactly. After my appointment, we went to lunch at the Senior Center. One of my friends there is very careful about what she eats, declining much of what is on the Center's menu and bringing her own creations of quinoa, kale, and other exotic ingredients. When I told her about the doctor's recommendation, she brightened and said, "I have that book!" She's having trouble reading after some eye surgeries and offered to lend me the book until she can see better. She brought it to me yesterday, and I don't think it's exactly the book the doctor was talking about. It's written by Dr. William Davis, the same man who wrote the original, but this is the cookbook.

At first I thought it wouldn't be of any help, but I started looking at it, and the first ninety pages give what is probably the Readers' Digest condensed version of the first book. The rest of the book consists of 150 wheat-free recipes along with some personal testimonials about the benefits of the program. It looks interesting, and David seems willing to give it a try, but it's not going to be simple.

First, I have a kitchen full of wheat products, and I'm not about to do a wholesale purge and throw bags of cereal and boxes of brownie mix in the trash. Second, I'm not sure where to find almond flour, ground flax seed, sucralose, and guar gum. Emory Food Mart just started carrying soy milk within the last few months. But I enjoy experimenting with new recipes, and I'm open to anything that might improve our health, so I'm going to give it a try. If nothing else, it should provide some interesting writing material. Stay tuned.

CHAPTER 75

Wheat Belly Update: Baby Steps – 3/15/14

Last week I wrote about the possibility of eliminating wheat from David's and my diet. I haven't made a lot of progress since then except in the area of awareness. I've been reading labels in my pantry, in my refrigerator, and on the shelves at the grocery store, and I'm amazed at where I find wheat. Soy sauce, of all things, contains wheat, and so do some frozen vegetables. The ingredients list on the California mix reads like this: broccoli, carrots, cauliflower, traces of wheat and soy. All mysteries are not found in Robert B. Parker novels.

David is becoming more aware along with me. Sometimes, as we sit down to dinner, he asks, "How much wheat is in this meal?" One evening the only thing that didn't contain the villainous grain was the sliced pear we shared.

Meal planning is already getting more challenging. As I use up wheat products, I'm not replacing them, but since I haven't yet found places to buy healthy alternatives, I'm using the unhealthy alternatives I have on hand. We have a full lunch at the Senior Center most weekdays, so we eat a lot of soup at night. David's supply of saltines ran out several days ago, so I've been serving him bread from the freezer. If I'm really going to do this, I need to hurry. The garlic bread ran out yesterday, and there are just a few Sister Schubert rolls left.

As I learn about ingredients, I'm also learning new things about my friends. After reading my original wheat belly post, one friend commented that she tried to go gluten free, but the alternatives caused her more grief than the wheat. Another friend called to say that she had lost fifteen pounds in three months by cutting out wheat and sugar. I think she also mentioned cutting out dairy, but after she mentioned sugar, my brain stopped listening and started shouting, "Let's not go overboard!"

The most helpful comment came from a friend who has been gluten-free for two years. She not only told me about her experiences, but she also gave me names of products she uses - products she buys at Walmart. I have no idea where the closest health food store is located, but there are five Walmarts within twenty to thirty miles of Emory.

After lunch today we stopped by the local Food Mart to pick up some milk and Blue Bell ice cream. I'll work on cutting out wheat first - sugar and dairy products can come later. While I was in the store, I checked the bread and cracker aisles. As I suspected, I didn't find any gluten-free products, but I found ground flax seeds on the baking aisle.

The Chinese philosopher Lao-tzu said "A journey of a thousand miles begins with one step." I'll need several other unusual ingredients before tackling some of the Wheat Belly recipes, but I have to start somewhere. Hopefully, in purchasing that bag of ground flax seeds, I've taken the first baby step toward better health for both David and me.

CHAPTER 76

Wheat Belly Update: The Next Step – 3/23/14

The progress is still slow in the quest to remove wheat from our diet, but there is progress nonetheless. In my last update, I mentioned that I found both whole and ground flaxseed at the local Food Mart. A few days ago I found coconut oil and a rice-based baking mix at the local Brookshire's. Purists will say that the processed rice flour is as bad as wheat flour, but I'm too new at this to be a purist.

I'm still in the process of using up the wheat products I have on hand, and that has resulted in some unusual meals. One night this week we had grilled cheese sandwiches on the last two hamburger buns. I'm trying to plan more meals that seem somewhat complete without bread. I also made some flax seed crackers to go with soup, so it may be a while before the frozen biscuits and rolls are gone.

The flax seed crackers turned out pretty well. We like the flavor, but they aren't crisp, and the texture is heavier than most crackers. The recipe said to line the pan with baking parchment, but I didn't have any. I used waxed paper instead, and that may have caused the crackers to retain more moisture than normal. I bought some parchment, and next time around, I may increase the baking time a bit. Maybe that will make a difference.

Stories and advice continue to come in from friends and even from friends I didn't know I had. I've developed an impressive list of products and reading material, and I'm planning a shopping trip to one of the surrounding Walmarts this week.

In addition to stories and advice, some friends are offering support of another kind. Last week at the Senior Center one of my friends who had obviously read my column called out to me as I walked by her with my lunch tray.

"Hey, Linda. Are you supposed to be eating that?"

I've written articles about the danger of knowing a writer. It's also dangerous to be a writer, especially if you lay your personal life out for the world to see. That's okay, though. The scrutiny of my friends keeps me honest and accountable. Hopefully, I'll have some results to report to you soon.

HUMOR

CHAPTER 77

Final Solutions - Graveyard Humor - 8/13/14

When I was younger, I thought operations and medications were the only subjects older people talked about. As I "matured," I realized that I was wrong. Sometimes we talk about our final wishes - how we want our earthly remains to be put to rest when we leave them behind. A couple of Sundays ago, several of us went to lunch after church. By the time our meal was finished, we had solved the world's problems, and our conversation drifted to more practical matters like the choice between burial and cremation.

One couple, while they took part in the discussion, remained non-committal about their personal plans. David plans to be buried at Uncle Sam's expense, thanks to his eleven years of service in the Navy. The rest of us plan to be cremated.

The wife of the first couple cringed at the mention of cremation. "I just can't stand the thought of it because burns are so painful." We all teased her for worrying about something she wouldn't be aware of, but feelings about such things are valid if not always logical.

I had not given much thought to the subject until several years ago when my son asked me to fill out something called Five Wishes. It's a document similar to a living will or an advanced directive, but with more detail. In the section that asks about funeral wishes, I asked for a simple cremation, for a tree to be planted in my memory, and for my ashes to be scattered around it.

The "cremation" couple had similar wishes. The wife wanted her ashes scattered in her garden, and the husband wanted his scattered in their pond so the catfish could eat them.

"Ewww," said his wife. "Then if we ate the fish, it would be like cannibalism!"

"It would be the same thing if we put yours in the garden," he reasoned.

Getting into the swing of the conversion, our squeamish friend had a suggestion. "I know," she said. "We can put them in your grandson's sand box. Then his mom can just say, 'Run on outside and play with Grandma!'"

Seniors may, at times, dwell on the darker aspects of life--but at least we have a sense of humor about it.

NOTE: For more information about Five Wishes, contact Aging with Dignity at 1-888-5947437 or www.agingwithdignity.org.

CHAPTER 78

When I Don't Have a Schedule – 11/30/14

Even though I'm retired, my life is somewhat structured, and most of my days have at least a loose schedule. It usually looks something like this: quiet time, breakfast, shower, personal work or part-time secretarial work at the church, lunch at the Senior Center, more church work or back home for house or yard work. There's lots of room for variation, but it keeps me more or less focused.

The Friday after Thanksgiving was an unusual day. There were no scheduled activities since both the church and the Senior Center were closed. I had written and scheduled my blog posts ahead of time, so I had no deadlines until Sunday. The refrigerator was full of leftovers from the day before, I didn't plan to participate in Black Friday, and there was nothing around the house that couldn't wait until Saturday, so I had a more or less free day.

I use a daily Bible Reading calendar as the guide for my morning reading. Sometimes I get a few days behind, especially during a holiday week that throws me a bit out of focus. Friday seemed like a perfect day to get caught up.

Just as I settled into my comfortable chair with my Bible-on-a-tablet, my phone reminded me that I needed to share updates. One of my secretarial duties is to post event reminders and updates on the church's Facebook page. I didn't want to post earlier in the week, so I had saved this week's updates and set the alarm. I put aside my Kindle and turned on my laptop.

Sometimes my computer is cranky in the morning, and Friday was one of those times. I clicked and pleaded, but the curser continued to spin. I admitted defeat and started the scans that would clean out all the cybertrash that clogs up the works. This process takes a while, so I went into the kitchen to start the coffee and set out cereal for breakfast.

For the next hour or so, my free, unscheduled day went something like this:

- The dishes in the dishwasher were clean, so I set the table from there and made a mental note to finish the job later.
- I ate breakfast and then settled down in the living room with a cup of coffee and my Kindle.
- After I read two chapters of Hebrews, I headed for the bathroom to take my morning vitamins.
- On the way, I stopped in the kitchen to leave my empty cup but decided to have a second cup instead. I returned to my chair and noticed that my computer had completed the scans and restarted.
- I surfed a bit while I drank my coffee, then I went back to the kitchen where I finished unloading and reloading the dishwasher.
- The absorbent mat on the counter was dirty, so I gather it and enough towels to make a load and went to the utility room.
- Once the towels were in the washing machine, I picked up an empty cereal box David had missed when he took out the

trash. I waded through several inches of dead leaves to get to the trash barrel - then, I grabbed the broom and swept the porch.
- When I was putting the broom away, I checked out the shelves against the wall. If I collected and hung the plastic bags I can't seem to throw away, I'd have space to store the empty canning jars that had been sitting on the kitchen counter.
- I was headed to the front bedroom to look for a picture hook when I noticed some wool socks I had hung over the shower curtain rod to dry.
- I grabbed the socks, found the hook, and dropped the socks on my bed.
- I returned to the utility room, mounted the bags, straightened the shelf, and put the jars in place.
- I headed toward the bathroom, but on the way, I noticed the socks and put them away.
- Then, I brushed my teeth, took my vitamins, and returned to the computer where I posted the church updates. It was 11:00 am, and I was still behind in my Bible reading.

CHAPTER 79

Four Christmas Gift Fails – 12/7/14

I don't do a lot of Christmas shopping any more, but when I do, I have fun. My budget is usually limited, so I don't feel pressured to find the perfect gift for each one on my list. Instead I shop the way Mom and I did when I was a kid. I go to a local store and wander through the aisles until something jumps out me. Regardless of how you shop, there are those gifts that simply fail.

The year I was sixteen, I couldn't wait to go Christmas shopping. I worked at Woolworth's making $1.10 an hour, and I was anxious to share my wealth. I don't remember most of what I bought, but I remember what I got for Mom - a frying pan.

Since Mom commuted to Dallas and didn't get home until 6:30, I cooked dinner most nights and was aware of the kitchen needs. We had a couple of skillets, but one had a wobbly handle and one had only a metal stub where the handle had once been. That's why, on my first December payday, I visited the kitchen section of Montgomery Ward and purchased a shiny new frying pan. That night I carefully wrapped it and put it under the tree. Then, buyer's remorse set in.

What was I thinking! Sure, we needed a new frying pan, but Mom would not be excited to see one on Christmas morning.

One night after Mom went to bed I sneaked the box out from under the tree, carefully unwrapped it, and removed the ill-advised gift. I re-wrapped the empty box and placed it back under the tree. The next day I returned the skillet and bought a cute pair of black shoes, and that night I completed my gift switcheroo. The shoes fit, and she loved them. I don't think I ever told her how close she came to getting a real failure of a Christmas present.

Several years later, Mom presented me with an odd gift. I had been married for four years but had not yet ventured into motherhood. We were spending Christmas with Mom and Dad, and I was very surprised when I opened my gift from her and found a very lacy nightgown. I'm sure I had a confused look on my face as I looked up - and then I saw the mischievous look on her face.

"I want a grandbaby!" she said. Needless to say, she was thrilled when she had a new grandson to play with the next Christmas.

When this grandson was four years old, all he wanted for Christmas was a Sit 'N Spin. Based on television advertising, he was convinced that the magical toy was the answer to all his dreams. When he came downstairs Christmas morning, his dream toy was sitting under the tree. His face lit up, and he ran over and plopped down on it. Nothing happened. He sat, but it didn't spin. His face fell and his eyes filled with tears.

"It doesn't work!" he wailed.

Once he let go of his unrealistic expectations and realized that the spinning required kid power, he spent many happy hours making himself dizzy. At that moment, however, the gift of his dreams was a total fail.

My fourth failed gift was to my mother-in-law - the one person you really want to impress. Mine was a wonderful woman, but her very specific tastes and her tendency to buy the things she wanted for herself made it hard to buy for her. One year, as the relatively new daughter-in-law, I had the bright idea to get her a spa day - a facial, a manicure, and a pedicure. She was pleased with her gift and looked forward to a new experience.

Unfortunately, the experience didn't live up to expectations. In fact, it turned out to be one of those gifts that keeps on giving. She developed a fungus under the nail of the big toe on her right foot. She lost the nail, and she had recurring problems with it for the rest of her life. As I said in the beginning, even the most discerning shopper sometimes experiences failure.

CHAPTER 80

The Downsizing of America – 1/13/15

Have you noticed that a lot of things in this country are getting smaller - and I'm not talking about the glaciers in Alaska or the coastline of California. I first became aware of this phenomenon a few years ago when my mother-in-law was making tuna salad for lunch.

"Linda," she asked as she opened a couple of cans, "why is the tuna so runny lately? I buy the same brand I've always bought, and it's mostly water."

I hadn't really paid that much attention, but she was right. I did a little investigating - actually, I read the label - and discovered that the same size can that once held six ounces of tuna now held only five. That was just the beginning.

Next, it was the cole slaw - the sixteen-ounce bag of shredded cabbage shrank to twelve. I had to rework my dressing recipe, and instead of being able to throw it together from memory, I had to deal with either fractions of measurements or soupy coleslaw. As if that weren't bad enough, the reduced size made only six servings instead of eight which doesn't work out evenly for a household of four.

And don't even get me started on the sweetened condensed milk. The fourteen-ounce can became eleven and a half ounces, and cream cheese had to be added to the lemon pie recipe to make it fit in the graham cracker crust.

The lunacy didn't stop with food products. A couple of months ago, when I was changing a roll of toilet paper, I realized that there was empty space on either side of the roll. I seem to remember a time when the roll fit snugly, so I did a little research - I posted on Facebook. I learned I wasn't the first to notice the shrinkage, and I learned how much smaller the average roll was now than it was in happier times. Unfortunately, I don't remember the specifics.

Then came last weekend, and it was almost too much. Not only have the mysterious *they* invaded my kitchen and my bathroom, but when I was getting dressed Saturday morning, I realized that no place is safe from their tinkering. I opened a new bottle of facial astringent and noticed it was a slightly different shape than the old one. I sighed and read the label - it was two ounces smaller.

So there you have the ugly truth. Someone is picking our pockets, not by raising the prices but by decreasing the sizes. I have heard financial advisors say that, when faced with a financial crisis, the answer is not to earn more but to need less. It seems that American manufacturers have heard this same advice and are taking care of the issue for us.

CHAPTER 81

Ten Things That Can Make You Feel Old (and what to do about them) – 1/25/15

Last week I wrote about feeling old. I received several comments from readers, so I decided I'd continue the topic by sharing a top ten list I posted on my blog a couple of years ago. It was originally inspired by an article from the AgingCare.com newsletter. The article contained some good information about exercise, diet, mental stimulation and other areas of concern, but I thought it omitted some rather obvious subjects. So here's my top ten list of things that can make you feel old and what to do about them.

1. Waiters and waitresses who automatically give you the senior discount.
   Tip only the ones who ask for proof of age, and we will eventually get them all trained.

2. Adult children who complain publicly about double chins and thinning hair.
Threaten to disinherit them unless they get a face lift and lie about their age.
3. Doctors who automatically refer to the number of years you've been alive when you complain about a new ache or pain.
Start a campaign to make the phrase "at your age" politically incorrect.
4. Shopping for clothes.
Do business only with stores that feature dressing rooms with flattering lighting and mirrors that show you only from the waist up. Also, buy only brands that mis-size their clothes to the low side. (Oh, look! I'm down to a size 6!)
5. Junk mail and spam that offer special discounts on scooter chairs and discreet delivery of incontinence supplies.
Write your congressman, demanding that he or she forget trivial matters like the national debt and focus on banning the ongoing effort to undermine our belief that we're still 25 years old.
6. When your arms aren't quite long enough to bring those last few lines of the contract into focus.
Write that same congressman about outlawing fine print.
7. When kids start making comments about your gray hair and wrinkles.
Remind the parents of these rug rats that children should be seen and not heard.
8. Sitting on a beach next to a group of twenty-somethings with Scarlett O'Hara waistlines and bikinis the size of postage stamps.
Cover your legs with a beach towel and offer the girls chocolate - lots of it.
9. Everyone at your high school reunion looks the way you remember their grandparents looking, and all the conversation

centers around ailments and Medicare supplements.
Don't go to high school reunions.
10. You discover that your first car is now considered an antique.
There is no remedy for this one.

As the years begin to pile up, remember what my brother Jim says: *Getting old is mandatory; growing up is not.* Stay young at heart.

CHAPTER 82

Bugs – Betcha Can't Eat Just One – 4/05/15

People sometimes give me ideas for columns, but unless I can come up with my own twist on a subject, I have trouble using these contributions. However, there's always the exception. A couple of weeks ago at the Senior Center, Billy Hollie handed me an item he had clipped from a magazine. I don't know which magazine, but the item was a question from a column called *Ask Dr. Bob*.

I keep hearing about foods made with crickets. Are they actually good for you?

My answer would have been, "That's just gross!"

Dr. Bob was a little more diplomatic. He said that whole crickets provide tasty snacks and that cricket flour is a greater source of protein than traditional foods. Bob went on to say that he bought crickets in open-air markets while he was on assignment in Darfur, Sudan. He said they have a nutty taste. He also said that, although crickets are not yet easily available, he predicts they will eventually offer a "great, eco-friendly option." I think I'll have to take his word on that.

Billy, on the other hand, seemed more than willing to consider the option. He asked me to research where he might purchase some of the crunchy crawlers. I assumed he wanted them for his own consumption, but judging by the twinkle in his eye, he might have some more mischievous purpose in mind.

The Internet revealed a few options. There were Crick-ettes Snacks, available in three tasty flavors: sour cream and onion, bacon and cheese, and salt and vinegar. Chocoholics can also buy chocolate covered crickets. I love chocolate, and the covering might disguise what is hiding underneath. Still, probably not.

I found a couple of sources for cricket flour, but it's really expensive. I also came across several resources for energy bars made with the flour. I haven't had a chance to talk with Billy yet. It will be interesting to see if he can, as Dr. Bob says, get past the *eww* factor.

CHAPTER 83

Is It "Smartphone Face or Just a Double Chin? – 4/14/15

Since I've passed the age of Medicare eligibility, I avoid mirrors as much as possible. I don't wear much make-up anymore. I hate the paste of foundation and powder that collects in the little lines that run from the sides of my nose to the corners of my mouth. On those rare occasions when I do put on a little bit of blush or lipstick, or when I style my hair, I focus on the area I'm working on and try to avoid looking at the rest.

Still, a mirror ambushes me occasionally, and I catch a full view of the laugh lines that have morphed into full blown crows' feet and the sagging jowls make me look a bit like Winston Churchill. Actually I look more like someone closer to home - my mother. When I catch an unexpected glimpse of myself, I sometimes think I'm looking at a portrait of her instead of an image of myself.

As if age and gravity weren't enough, there is now a new factor that may add to the loose, saggy skin between my chin and collarbones. It's called *smartphone face*. One Internet pundit defined the new phenomenon this way: *a drooping jaw-line and saggy jowls caused by neck muscles that have been shortened from constantly looking down at a smartphone or similar device.*

This new phone face woe warranted an article in the New York Post. According to the author, Amber Sutherland, some New Yorkers have shrugged off the potential danger, choosing not to worry about it. I agree with Amber. I'm not sure if it is a desire on my part to age gracefully and accept the face God has given me or if it's the fact that I don't have the money to do anything about it, but I try not to worry about it either.

If, however, you choose to fight nature, there are things you can try. Some options are facelifts, chin filler injections, Botox, and liposuction. If those solutions are too drastic, you might consider simply holding your phone at shoulder level when reading or texting. I don't know if this will help your double chin, but if you do it consistently, you might actually tighten up those sagging triceps a bit.

CHAPTER 84

Ten Ways to Know You're Getting Older – 4/19/15

The most obvious way to know you're getting older is to have another birthday. I had one last week, and since it was impossible to ignore the event, I decided to embrace it in this week's column. Following are ten additional ways to know you are getting older.

1. Your friendly Medicare supplement carrier notifies you that your health insurance premium will increase again. *Mine went up approximately 15%.*
2. Sales clerks, waiters and waitresses give you the senior discount without asking. *We went to A.J.s for my birthday dinner, and we didn't have to show proof of age to get the senior buffet.*
3. You're much more likely to ask your friends to recommend a doctor than a babysitter. *If you doubt this one, just drop by the Senior Center and listen to the conversations.*
4. When your friends say *It's getting close to nap time,* they're not talking about the grandkids. *In the interest of full disclosure, it's not just my friends who say that.*

5. You have more prescription bottles than perfume bottles in your bathroom. *These bottles and their contents is also a popular topic of conversation at the Center.*
6. You can say *been there and done that* to, well, to almost everything. *I have discovered that, when you get too old to go there and do that, you can always write about it.*
7. The "noise" your kids listened to as teenagers is now played on the golden oldies stations. *When the floors of my house vibrated with the sounds of Metallica and Pearl Jam, I never thought of them as classics material.*
8. You can truthfully answer "yes" to every one of the "do you remember" emails and Facebook posts. *Unfortunately, the older you get, the more questionable the remembering part becomes.*
9. Your baby is worrying about his thinning hair and the wattle under his chin. *Mine finally gave up fighting the hair loss and shaved his head. I'm not sure what he's doing about the wattle.*
10. You receive an invitation to you 50th high school reunion. *Mine is in October.*

CHAPTER 85

The Silliness of Soap – 5/17/15

I was cleaning the bathroom one morning when my mind began to wander. Scrubbing toilets frees plenty of brain power for thinking, so I thought about soap. Soap didn't just pop into my mind for no reason. It came up as I a searched the utility room for a particular kind of cleanser to combat a particularly unsightly stain. I was amazed at the array of choices. My mind chased one rabbit after another, the writer overcame the housewife (not much of a contest), and I ended up at the computer.

According to Dictionary.com, soap is *a substance used for washing and cleansing purposes, usually made by treating a fat with an alkali...,blah, blah, blah*. Wikipedia said the earliest recorded evidence of soap came from Babylon around 2800 BC. The formula was simple: water, alkali and oil. My curiosity was aroused, so I took a home inventory. Here are the results in no particular order.

Utility Room:

- degreaser

- spot and stain removal treatments for laundry
- blue glass cleaner and pink chrome and glass cleaner
- mildew remover
- lime, rust and calcium remover
- powdered and liquid sink scrubbers
- disinfectant wipes
- bathroom spray cleaner
- toilet bowl cleaner
- carpet and upholstery cleaner
- regular and delicate laundry detergent
- brass cleaner and brass, chrome and metal polish
- concentrated all-purpose cleaner
- ammonia all-purpose cleaner
- dishwasher cleaner

Kitchen:

- liquid hand soap
- dishwashing liquid
- dishwasher detergent
- steel wool soap pads

Bathroom:

- anti-bacterial deep cleansing liquid hand soap
- bar soap
- "wet wipes" for cleaning glasses and other lenses
- shaving soap
- saddle soap (we don't have saddles, but David uses it on his boots)
- poison ivy soap (not to wash the poison ivy, but to wash us when we get exposed which is often around here)

- toothpaste (that's a kind of soap, isn't it)
- bath soak for dry skin
- liquid body wash
- face scrub
- shampoo - regular, dandruff and some disgusting stuff with coal tar for really bad dandruff. At one time my bathroom also sported shampoos for color-treated and dry hair, but since my hair is now naturally highlighted by age, I've given those up. I am, however, considering something for thinning, limp hair.

We've come a long way since 2800 BC. How did soap evolve from a simple solution of three ingredients to a mind-boggling array of products and choices? Have we become dirtier through the ages, or have we become cleaner? Have we become intelligent enough to know that each cleaning job requires a different product, or have we fallen prey to Madison Avenue hype because, as they used to say on Saturday Night Live, "we'll believe anything?" I'll have to leave the answers to those questions to you. If I told you what I really think, I'd have to wash my mouth out with soap.

CHAPTER 86

Senior Humor – 10/19/15

November is National Family Caregiver Month. In honor of all the families who devote themselves to the care of loved ones, many of whom are elderly, I've decided to devote my columns in the next few weeks to some stories about the lighter side of both aging and caregiving.

I often quote Bette Davis who said that getting old is not for sissies. Neither is caregiving. Getting older and caring for the elderly are not laughing matters, but sometimes there are moments. In fact, seeing the humor is a great defense against the dark side. When I co-facilitated a caregiver support group several years ago, I collected a little senior humor from the Internet and sometimes opened meetings with a joke or two to lighten the mood and take our minds off the latest caregiving crisis. Here are a few of my favorites.

The nice thing about being senile is you can hide your own Easter eggs.

Mom never hid her own eggs, but she once hid her purse with all her insurance and identification cards in it, and it took me two weeks to find it.

Reporters interviewing a 104-year-old woman:
"And what do you think is the best thing about being 104?" the reporter said.
"No peer pressure."

Mom lived a lot of her life worrying about what people thought of her. Alzheimer's is a senseless and insidious disease, but if it has a silver lining, it is that it took away Mom's fears and social anxieties. As her disease progress, she became a party girl, the life of the party, the sweet little lady with the constant smile and the ready hug who doesn't worry at all about peer pressure.

I've sure gotten old! I've had two bypass surgeries, a hip replacement, new knees, fought prostate cancer and diabetes. I'm half blind, can't hear anything quieter than a jet engine, take 40 different medications that make me dizzy, winded, and subject to blackouts. I have bouts with dementia, have poor circulation, and can hardly feel my hands and feet anymore. I can't remember if I'm 85 or 92. I've lost all my friends, but, thank God, I still have my driver's license.

This one was too close to the truth to be funny. When we moved to Florida, we all made a trip to the driver's license office. I had already taken the car keys away from Mom and Dad, but they both still had their Texas licenses. My hope was that the State of Florida would be my ally in making their non-driving status official. It was no problem with Mom. She was taking some dementia medications that disqualified her, so the State issued her a picture I.D. Not so with Dad. He hobbled up to the counter with the aid of his 4-footed cane and struggled to find his old license in his wallet. He finally gave up and asked me to find it for him. In spite of all of that, he walked out with a Florida license. The one saving grace was that he couldn't get far without the keys.

Just before the funeral services, the undertaker approached the elderly widow.

"How old was your husband?" he said.

"'98," she said. "Two years older than me."

"So you're 96," the undertaker said.

She smiled and said, "Hardly worth going home, is it?"

One thing we talked about a lot in our support group was finishing well. If we can live in such a way that we can approach the finish line with the humor and aplomb of this elderly lady, and if we can help our loved ones do the same, we will have finished well.

CHAPTER 87

More Senior Humor – 10/25/15

Last week I began celebrating National Family Caregiver Month a little early by sharing a few stories about the lighter side of both aging and caregiving. Here are a few more.

Grandma decided to put a jigsaw puzzle together, so she grabbed the box and poured the pieces out on the table. After a while, she began to get frustrated and called Grandpa.

"George, can you come in here and give me a hand."

"Honey, what's wrong?"

"I'm trying to put this puzzle together, but none of the pieces fit."

"Well, look at the picture on the box and tell me what it looks like."

"Okay. The background is blue, and there's a tiger on it."

"Right. Now let's put the cornflakes back in the box."

Mom was not a fan of jigsaw puzzles, so we never had this problem, but she did have problems with her cereal. I've never been one to stand over a hot stove early in the morning, so we usually starts the day with cereal, coffee and maybe fruit. Mom and Dad always woke up later than we did, so I would leave the cereal, bowls, spoons, and sweetener on the table and let them take care of themselves.

This worked out well for a while, but even that simple task soon became too much for Mom. She sometimes forgot to pour milk into her bowl, and I'd find her crunching on really dry cereal or see her scraping her bowl, trying to get the dry sweetener off the bottom. I encouraged Dad to oversee her breakfast preparation, but he was doing well to see to his own meal.

One day I came in to clean up their post-breakfast mess and found fifteen or so empty pink packages lying on the table. She had emptied every package of sweetener into her bowl. I knew then it was time for me to get involved in yet another aspect of her life and help her "put the cornflakes back in the box."

Returning home from work, the elderly lady was shocked to find her house ransacked and burglarized. She telephoned the police at once and reported the crime. The police dispatcher broadcast the call, and a K-9 unit patrolling nearby was the first to respond. As the officer approached the house with his dog on a leash, the lady ran out on the porch, shuddered at the sight of the cop and his dog, and sat down on the steps. Putting her face in her hands, she burst into tears.

"I come home to find all my possessions stolen. I call the police for help, and what do they do? They send me a BLIND policeman!"

I've never experienced a burglary, but Mom and I had a close call when I was in my early teens. Dad worked nights and my older brother Jim was away at college, so Mom and I were often home alone. One night she woke me, saying someone was scratching on the window screen in her bedroom. We clung to each other, staring at the window, and suddenly a shadow passed across the shade. I called Dad, and he called the police. Within minutes a car pull up in front of the house and flashlights criss-crossed the yard as Mesquite's finest investigated. Then, we heard a knock on the door.

"We didn't find anything, Ma'am, but we'll have a car drive by here frequently for the rest of the night."

When Dad arrived at home the next morning, he found us still huddled together under the covers. He immediately went out to investigate and came back inside laughing.

"I didn't find any footprints, but I did find some evidence. There were rat droppings on the window sill."

A young man wanted to do something special for his grandmother, so he decided to take her to a football game. She had never been to one before, but he thought she would enjoy all the noise and excitement. They had great seats on the fifty yard line, and their team won. After the game, he asked how she liked it.

"Oh, it was great," she said, "especially the tight pants and all the big muscles. But I just don't understand why they were killing each other over such a trivial thing."

"What do you mean, Grandma?"

"Well, they flipped a coin, one team got it and then for the rest of the game they kept screaming, 'Get the quarterback! Get the quarterback!' I mean, after all, it was only twenty-five cents."

On Sunday afternoons, you could always find Mom and Dad in front of the TV, rooting for the Cowboys. They thought Roger Staubach hung the moon, and they agreed with Don Meredith that Texas Stadium was built with a hole in the roof so God could watch His team.

A lot of things changed through the years, but until they lost interest in television altogether, they could still be found on Sunday afternoons in front of the TV, rooting for the 'Boys. They didn't remember the names of the players, and they fell asleep between touchdowns, but they were always Cowboy fans.

CHAPTER 88

There's a National Month for Everything – 11/1/15

It's true. There seems to be a national day, week, or month for almost anything you can think of. The last two weeks I've mentioned that November is National Caregiver Month, but November is also National Novel Writing Month. I've been working on, if not the great American novel, at least a project that has interested me for quite a while, but I've only managed to get a little over 6,000 words actually written. I've decided to use the motivation and peer pressure of NaNoWriMo and to focus my keyboard time on getting a complete rough draft into the computer. With that in mind, instead of a *real* column, here's one more week of stories about the lighter side of aging and caregiving.

An older woman went into a store to buy curtains.

She approached the salesman and said, "I want those pink curtains in the display, but I need them customized to fit my computer screen."

"Ma'am," said the salesman, "I've worked here for 20 years, and I've never had a request like that. Why do you need curtains for your computer?"

"Hellooo," said the woman. "I have windows!"

Many of us older people don't understand electronics as well as we'd like to. The wisdom of seniors is *if you need tech support, call your grandkids.* My Aunt Fay is an exception. She is 94 and has used her computer to take a couple of college courses, compile a history of her church, research the genealogy of her family, and keep in touch with her family by e-mail. She was on Facebook for a while, but she decided it was a bit racy for her, so she closed her account. She might ask for help in learning to use the Dragon software her daughter bought her so she can write the family history, but she would never put curtains on her computer screen!

A very elderly gentleman walked into an upscale cocktail lounge. He was very well dressed, his hair was well groomed, he had on a great looking suit with a flower in his lapel, and he smelled slightly of a good after shave. He spotted a nice-looking older woman seated at the bar next to an empty stool. He walked over, sat down, ordered a drink, and turned to her.

"So tell me," he said with a smile. "Do I come here often?"

There's an old saying that goes *just because there's snow on the roof doesn't mean there isn't fire in the furnace.* Mom wasn't interested in finding a boyfriend after Dad died, but that's not always the case. The Senior Center here in Emory has seen three romances bloom and lead to the altar in the last few years.

A student nurse was told that the patient in Room 212 was being discharged and was ready to be escorted to his vehicle. Hospital regulations required a wheelchair for patients being discharged, so she found one that wasn't being used and went to the room. An elderly gentleman was dressed and sitting on the bed with a suitcase at his feet. He insisted he didn't need her help to leave the hospital, but after a chat about rules being rules, he reluctantly let her wheel him to the elevator. On the way down, she asked him if his wife was meeting him.

"I don't know", he said. "She's still upstairs in the bathroom changing out of her hospital gown."

When I first heard this story, I could picture this happening to Dad. He and Mom looked at those in the medical profession as being a step or two above us common folks. They never doubted or asked questions, and they never went against doctor's orders unless the orders involved exercising or cutting down on Blue Bell.

A group of senior citizens was taking an overseas tour, and they were spending several days in London. On their first day there, the tour guide loaded them aboard a double-decker bus for a tour of the city.

The seniors on the lower level were partying and having a great time, when they realized there was no noise coming from upstairs.

The tour guide decided to go up and investigate. When he reached the top, he found all the passengers frozen in fear, staring straight ahead, clutching the armrests with white knuckles.

"What's going on up here?" he said. "Everyone is having a great time downstairs."

"Yeah," said a man in the front row. "But you've got a driver!"

I never had the chance to travel overseas with Mom and Dad, but we traveled with them a lot in the motorhome. Their child-like trust kept them from being afraid, even at times when fear might have been in order - like when David and I traded drivers while the RV was still in motion - but that's a story for another time.

WRITING

CHAPTER 89

Anaiah Press Accepted My Memoir: Will Publication Make a Difference – 1/19/14

A couple of weeks ago I signed a piece of paper, and my life changed. Oh, it didn't really change all that much. We still ate a simple dinner at home and watched a movie on TV. When I looked in the mirror the next morning, I didn't look any different, and I sat in the same chair in the living room when I had my quiet time. And when I turned on the computer and prepared to write, I was faced with the same blank screen, staring at me and daring me to find the words. And yet it was different.

The first post I published when I started my blog over two years ago was called "My Book." It gave a bit of the history of the book, how it started as a travel journal, penned in a spiral notebook. It told a little bit about the seven-week RV trip my husband and I took with my mom and dad, both of whom had dementia and who lived with us. It told of the drama and hilarity that ensue when two people who don't know much about RV travel and two people who don't know much about anything spend fifty-three days inside a 400-square-foot box on wheels. It also told about the fourteen edits. But it didn't tell about the sense of accomplishment and the doubts, the encouragement and the rejections, the hopes and the fears. And it didn't tell what a difference a signature on a piece of paper, on a publication agreement, can make.

This is not a fairy tale ending, though - not the happily ever after of the stories of my childhood. There will be editorial criticisms and re-writes, there may be delays and glitches, there will be good reviews and bad ones. But, for now, someone has seen enough value in my efforts to help me share them. My hope is that those who eventually read my book will be encouraged, inspired, or amused, and that my words will make a difference.

Anaiah Press is a Christian digital-first publishing house dedicated to presenting quality faith-based fiction and nonfiction books to the public. A LONG AND WINDING ROAD: A Caregiver's Tale of Life, Love, and Chaos will be released July 1, 2014.

CHAPTER 90

The Glamour of Being an Author – 5/19/14

I signed my first autographs as an author Saturday. If you close your eyes and try to picture it, you might envision me surrounded by adoring fans who are vying for my attention. Since my book hasn't been released yet, and when it is released, it will initially be in ebook form, scraps of paper, napkins, and t-shirts are being waved at me in the hope of getting my coveted signature. Well, it wasn't quite like that.

I got an email from Anaiah Press a couple of weeks ago telling me they were sending several small posters. I was asked to sign and return them so they could be used as giveaways in connection with the upcoming release. The package arrived shortly after David and I left to visit his mom in Louisiana, and by the time we returned home, it had been waiting in the Post Office for almost a week. I told my editor I had the posters and would try to get them back in the mail on Friday. It didn't happen.

I had intended to make the signing into a kind of mini event. I planned to dress presentably and get David to snap a few pictures that I might use in my blog or some other form of publicity. Then, Saturday morning, I saw the unsigned posters, still lying on the Queen Anne chair in the corner of the living room. Both my garden and my house were in need of my attention, and that didn't leave much time for a photo op. Besides, David was leaving in a few minutes for a men's breakfast, and if I hurried, I could get him to mail the package while he was out.

So, instead of a semi-glamorous poster-signing, I stood at the dining room table, dressed in flannel house pants, fuzzy house shoes, my son's old water polo t-shirt, and David's sweat jacket while I signed my first five professional autographs. Then, I donned my work jeans, my ratty tennis shoes, and my straw hat and spent several hours doing battle with weeds.

Writing can be a lonely vocation, sitting in a quiet corner, lost in the world that swirls around inside your head. In this day of electronic communications, a writer seldom meets her readers face to face, and few of us are well-known enough to create excitement over our signatures. But if we're lucky, occasionally we'll get an email or a comment telling us how something we wrote amused, encouraged, or inspired someone - that's glamorous enough for me.

CHAPTER 91

Waiting Room Characters and Stories – 6/14/14

I spent a lot of time waiting this week, sitting patiently on the fourth floor of the VA hospital in Bonham while David had his eyes checked on Thursday and had a skin cancer removed on Friday. He tried to get the appointments on the same day, but large organizations are not always set up for the convenience of the end user.

The waiting room was more crowded than usual on Friday. The small groups that were hanging around in the long, narrow room had left empty chairs between themselves and the next group so they didn't invade one another's personal space. In order that David and I could sit together and leave the requisite empty chair, I ended up tucked in a corner behind an oscillating fan. The situation wasn't bad, though. The fan wasn't turned on, so I didn't have to dodge the swiveling head, and I had a good view of the room.

As usual, I brought a book to help pass the time, and I read some - but, like most writers do, I spent a lot of time people-watching. Two men were carrying on a conversation across the middle of the room - actually one was talking and one was listening. As veterans are likely to do, the talker was telling stories of his time in the service. A nurse called his name shortly after we arrived, and he walked down the hall with her, leaving a momentary silence behind him. Judging by the volume of his voice, I'm guessing he was having his hearing checked.

A small family group sat across from me. At first, it was an elderly man and his daughter. Then, when they were told it would be a while longer before the dermatologist could get to him, she left. When she came back a little while later, she had her two grandchildren with her. They each had a backpack and looked dressed for an afternoon of playing with Grandma. However, she explained to her dad that they were worried about him and wanted to keep him company before they went to play. While they waited, they busied themselves with Grandma's iPhone and toys from their backpacks, but they glanced at Grandpa from time to time to make sure he was okay. When he was called back, they looked a little worried, and they scooted together and sat a little closer to Grandma. When he came back out a few minutes later, the little girl ran to his side. She cut her eyes up at him and asked if it hurt. When he said no, she looked relieved and ran over to push the elevator button.

As I watched the people come and go, I thought about a couple I'd seen in the same waiting room a couple of years before. They sat off to one side, her arm linked through his, their heads close together, chatting quietly. I'm not one to eaves drop, and I was pretty absorbed in a book, but something grabbed my attention. I don't know if it was the emphasis she placed on the words or the words themselves.

"Marry me," she said, and then repeated herself several times in rapid succession.

"I love you too much to marry you," he said with a smile in his voice.

This exchange was repeated a couple of times, and then their conversation subsided to its previously low levels. I got the feeling it was a conversation they often had, always with the same results. When the nurse called him back to the examining room, she went with him, her arm still linked through his.

Once David's name was called, it didn't take long for the doctor to scrape and burn the small place on his shoulder. On the way home, we watched the clouds and speculated as to whether it had rained on our garden while we were gone, and we stopped in Leonard for Blizzards. The outing took most of the day, and for anyone who's not a collector of characters and stories, it might have been boring. But I find life pretty entertaining, and it's a good thing. David has to go back again in three months.

CHAPTER 92

Tributes to Those We Love – 6/29/14

Last week, I attended an unusual funeral. To be sure, there were some tears and some evidence of sadness, but mostly it was a joyful celebration of a life well lived and a loving tribute to a man who was well loved. One of the first things I noticed was a large floral arrangement that depicted a man on an orange riding lawn mower. Next, I noticed that when the extended family filed into the sanctuary, most of them had on something red.

The daughter of the departed read the eulogy. She began with the traditional statistics—dates of birth, marriage, death, and also the names of survivors. From there, she went on to tell her father's life story. She told of his spiritual journey from a rough-edged man of the world to a devoted follower of Jesus. Assisted by her daughters and nieces, she told stories that were both funny and touching—and she explained the flower arrangement and the color choices. As his health declined and walking became difficult, her father used his riding mower to keep tabs on his beloved homestead. His orange four-wheeler, as he called the mower, became a personal trademark along with the color red. Red was his favorite color because he said it reminded him of the blood of Jesus.

A celebratory memorial service can be a wonderful tribute, but there are also other ways of expressing love and appreciation to those we value. For centuries artists have paid tribute to people of value through sculpture, painting, and other art forms. Modern technology now allows us to immortalize each other through photography and other visual imagery. In addition to artistic tributes, we can honor those we love with written tributes and what I like to call lifestyle tributes.

My first close encounter with written tributes was several years ago when I was involved in a caregiver support group. At one point, we devoted several meetings to the topic, and I was surprised to discover that written tributes can sometimes be more important to the writer than to the honoree. Since many of our loved ones were afflicted by some sort of dementia, reading or presenting a letter or framed document to them would have been confusing. However, the writing process helped the caregiver focus on the more positive aspects of her loved one. Remembering who the person was before age, infirmity, and dementia turned them into an angry, messy, uncooperative patient sometimes brought a kind of closure and a sense of relief. Often, comfort and healing came with the preparation of a tribute and by sharing it with the group.

Lifestyle tributes can help restore a sense of control that is taken away after years of dealing with uncontrollable situations. Some caregivers have become advocates, either against the disease that took their loved one or for causes that were important to them. I'm not much of an activist, but my writing has become, in part, a lifestyle tribute to Mom and Dad. When something I write encourages caregivers and others who are in difficult situations, it seems to give some meaning to the otherwise meaningless struggle that defined the last years of Mom and Dad's lives.

Tributes can take many forms. Regardless of which form you choose, finding a way to show honor and respect to one you love is an important part of letting go and saying good-bye.

CHAPTER 93

Five Ways to Write a Memoir without Being Disowned – 8/17/14

Last week the *Leader* published a story about my recently released book. When Anaiah Press posted the first chapter of my memoir as a teaser, I got some nice feedback and also some interesting questions, mostly about how I found the courage to write a memoir. On the chance that some of my readers are considering writing a book about their family friends, I thought I'd share some of my thoughts.

Know your motives
Why are you writing your story? Do you have a purpose in mind, or do you just want to vent and air your dirty laundry? There is a market for both types of memoir, but the first is less likely to get you disowned.

When I first became a caregiver, my aunt suggested I keep a journal. At first, it was a place to vent when things got tense, but then I got brave and shared a few things on Facebook. People sometimes laughed or cried with me, and some said, "Thanks, I thought I was the only one." By the time I began writing my memoir, I had a purpose - to encourage, amuse, and maybe even inspire other caregivers. Hopefully, I haven't stepped on too many toes in the process.

Tell your own story

If you've ever studied conflict resolution, you're probably familiar with *I* messages. In any disagreement, it is important to speak about your own actions and feelings instead of assigning blame to someone else. *I felt abandoned when I didn't know where you went after work* instead of *You always go off without telling me where you're going.* In writing my memoir, I tried to tell my own story and leave others to tell theirs.

When I did cross over into a really personal story about someone else - like my son Christian's struggle with depression or one of my brother Jim's major clashes with Dad - I asked for their approval of what I wrote. The exceptions were Mom and Dad. They were very private people and would probably have been embarrassed by having people read about them. They were too far into their dementia to understand, though, so I didn't ask. After lots of prayer and consultation with people who loved all of us, I decided that helping others through their story somehow gave meaning to their struggles. I hope they agree or at least will have forgiven me by the time I see them again.

Make your characters likeable

After Anaiah picked up my book, I began working with Jessica Schmeidler, my talented and sensitive editor. As the reality of being published set in, I began to worry about the legal and ethical side of writing about real people. I asked her if I should contact each person I mentioned, use pseudonyms, or just take my chances. She said I should do whatever made me feel comfortable but that she didn't see any problems. "I like all your characters," she said, "so I don't see why anyone would be offended." In writing a memoir, a writer is not creating characters. However, she does have the ability to make her characters sympathetic or not, depending on how she presents them.

Forgive before you write

There is a verse in the Bible that addresses this - well, sort of.

Therefore, if you are offering your gift at the altar and there remember that your brother or sister has something against you, leave your gift there in front of the altar. First go and be reconciled to them; then come and offer your gift. Matthew 5:23-24

My advice would be, before you sit down to write about a person who has hurt you in some way, be sure you have forgiven that person before you put your hands on the keyboard. As the author, you have complete control and can tell your story so that your readers will understand without a doubt who was the injured party and who the villain was, but you also have to be sure you're prepared to accept the consequences. You have to decide if vindication is worth becoming the pariah of the family.

Speak the truth in love

Finally, whatever you choose to write, tell the truth as lovingly as you can. At some point in my caregiving journey, Mom and Dad became The Kids. It was a loving term that I used with friends and family who knew my situation. As Jessica and I worked on polishing my writing, I raised the question of whether "The Kids" might be considered disrespectful and offensive to some of my readers. I even wrote a blog post about it that included a poll. The responses to the poll were few, but the majority said *Yes* it was disrespectful. When I discussed the issue with both my husband and my pastor, they were conflicted. Both said their first reaction was *Yes*, but knowing me and how I much I loved my parents, they knew there was no disrespect involved. Jessica and I tweaked my story to make my intent clear, but she was not worried. "Linda, your love and care for your parents is so obvious that I don't think anyone will misunderstand."

If the author of a memoir skirts the truth in order to spare feelings, her story will not ring true. On the other hand, as she tells the truth, she must do so with love.

CHAPTER 94

On Being a Celebrity – 2/8/15

David and I made the front page of the newspaper last week. It was a small article announcing my upcoming book signing, and it included a picture of the two of us. Since then, we've encountered part of the fifteen minutes of fame Andy Warhol predicted everyone would experience in the modern world.

A lot of people at the Senior Center commented on the article and the picture. Most of them congratulated me and asked questions about the book - and quite a few of them asked David how it felt to be a celebrity husband. He was very gracious about the teasing.

In addition to being a celebrity, I go the school once a week to visit with one of the students. Last week, after my visit, I was sitting in the office doing the after-visit paperwork when a teacher came through to pick up a copy of the *Leader*. After she picked up her paper and dropped her fifty cents into the cup, she glanced at the front page and then looked at me with a grin.

"Well, look whose picture is in the paper. We have a celebrity in our midst!"

I smiled back self-consciously and said, "Yeah, well." I have a way with words.

Sunday morning at church several more people mentioned the article and said they planned to be at the signing. It's nice to know that David and I won't be there all by ourselves. A couple of people also shared their own aspirations to write a book and asked if they could contact me for advice. I assured them that I'd be glad to share what I know, which shouldn't take long.

Later that day, at our SISTAs meeting, one of my friends brought me her copy of the paper in case I wanted to send it to my son. Apparently, in addition to the front page article, she also read my City Girl column. In case you missed it, I wrote about how important the little things are. As an example, I told about how cutting bread out of our diet has led to a shortage of twisties. I also told about how touched I was when Margaret at the Senior Center saved the twisties from the hamburger buns for me.

When my friend arrived at the meeting, I was in the kitchen where we were working on casseroles to replenish the emergency supply we keep in the church freezer. She laid the newspaper on top of my Bible which I had left on one of the tables. My Bible isn't hard to find. It has a hot pink cover with a very blingy cross on the front, but that's another story. When I saw the newspaper, I noticed there was an envelope on top of it with my name on it. I thought it might be a congratulations card, but when I saw what it was, I started laughing. It was full of twisties.

Occasionally, when people find out that my book has been published, they say something like *Remember the little people.* I can't promise to always remember everyone's name. At my age, the mental rolodex begins to slip a bit. Regardless of whatever limited celebrity status I might attain, though, I'm pretty sure I'll always remember the little things.

CHAPTER 95

Hiding In the Luggage – 3/1/15

The last time Darren Brumit brought the morning message at Believers', he preached about the rise and fall of King Saul as told in 1 Samuel. The part that stood out to me was a small story in Chapter 10.

Saul was sent to find some lost donkeys. On the way, he met the Prophet Samuel who told him he had been chosen by God to be the king of Israel. Saul was reluctant, protesting that he was just a small town boy - not really king material. Later, when Samuel was ready to crown him publicly, Saul was found hiding in the luggage. I guess it was hard for him to move out of his comfort zone and onto center stage.

Not many of us are divinely anointed to rule a nation, but each of us is sometimes called out of our comfort zone. I've been out of my comfort zone a lot lately, especially the last couple of weeks. I'm basically a quiet, private person, which may sound strange coming from someone who writes extensively about her private life. Still, it's one thing to sit alone at a keyboard and another to stand in front of a group and talk about yourself. That's what I did Saturday at my first official book signing.

It's not as if I haven't been in front of people before. For sixteen years, I worked for a design and manufacturing company. I sometimes gave product demonstrations and sales seminars at trade shows and sales meetings. However, selling yourself and your own work is a completely different experience. On the other hand, successful writers are known, not as best-writing authors, but as best-selling authors, so you move out of your comfort zone and into the spotlight.

The planning stages for the signing were easy - designing a flyer, ordering business cards, planning what to serve. Then, it became a little more difficult. I asked people to put up my flyers, and I talked with people face-to-face about my writing. I began to wonder what I had gotten myself into and if there was any way out.

It reminded me of an experience at camp a couple of summers ago. We took the kids swimming every day, and they loved it when the counselors went in with them, especially if we went off the zip line into the pond. I avoided it the first day by going down the big slide, but the second day, my girls yelled at me from the top of the zip line ladder, and there was no escape. I had watched others take the walk of shame back down the ladder when their courage failed, so I tried not think about it too much and just put one foot in front of the other. When I reached the top, the attendant held out the grab bar. I took it, made a wise remark, and stepped off the platform. I screamed all the way down, but I survived.

As Saturday approached, I used the same tactic. I took one step at a time, trying not to think too much ahead. With the bad weather, I thought about canceling, but I had publicized pretty widely. Besides, I had lots of cookies.

The event was in the Meadows Room at the library, and as we set up Friday afternoon, I felt an odd sense of calm. Everything was falling into place, and I thought, *I can do this*. Saturday morning, I was excited but peaceful. I visited with friends, and when the time came for me to talk about and read from my book, I did what I had come to do. I don't know how I'll feel next time, but at least for this first signing, I didn't even look for a pile of luggage.

LOOKING BACK

CHAPTER 96

Beatlemania Affected Even Small Town Texas – 2/08/14

To coincide with the 50th anniversary of the Beatles' appearance on the Ed Sullivan show, Yahoo asked some of their contributors who remember the event to write first-person accounts about how that appearance helped spark changes across the nation. Here's what I wrote.

I was a 16-year-old high school junior in Mesquite, Texas when the Beatles burst into the living rooms of America on the Ed Sullivan show. Mesquite was a sleepy bedroom community southeast of Dallas that was relatively untouched by the outside world, but even Mesquite felt the effects of Beatlemania.

The Ed Sullivan Show

I didn't see the show. Mesquite was only a couple of generations removed from its farming roots, and social activities were usually connected with high school sports, church, or family. Sunday nights at my church included not only a worship service but also youth choir practice and fellowship, so The Ed Sullivan Show wasn't part of my routine. But it wasn't long before I began to see changes in hair styles and footwear and to hear changes in the music played by local musicians.

Hair Styles
Although we were only thirty miles from Dallas, Mesquite wasn't exactly a fashion center, so the boys at school didn't start growing mop tops immediately. But within a few months, waxed flat tops and greasy-kid-stuff hair styles were giving way to looser, longer looks. By the time I went away to college in 1965, very few male ears or foreheads were visible. My older brother was married and in the Marines by this time, so we escaped the war of the haircut that went on in the homes of many of my friends.

Footwear
Before the English Invasion, a few of the Future Businessmen wore lace-up shoes and a few of the Future Farmers wore cowboy boots, but most of the boys in town wore loafers. The change in shoe styles came a little slower than the change in haircuts, but when I came home from college on weekends, I began to see a few ankle boots with Cuban heels and pointed toes.

Music
The music of the Beatles had a noticeable effect at the University of North Texas where I attended college. The Beatles took rock music from the simple 1-4-5 chord structure early rockers adopted from their gospel and country roots and moved it into a complex musical structure that intrigued even the most militant music snob. UNT is noted for its music program, especially its jazz studies, but Beatles cover bands sprang up all over campus as musicians experimented with new chord structures, electronic enhancements, and

instrumentation that went well beyond the traditional three guitars and a drum set. I had a couple of dates with the bassist from one of these bands, and I even went with him to one of his gigs. The relationship didn't last long, but being "with the band" was a bold step for a girl from Mesquite.

Attitudes

The Beatles' appearance on The Ed Sullivan Show didn't change small town Texas overnight, but it opened our eyes to new possibilities. Seeing what was going on outside our city limits planted seeds of restlessness that led us to break with tradition. It gave us a look at what the rest of the world was doing, and Sunday night youth fellowship was never quite the same.

CHAPTER 97

Healthcare - Then and Now – 7/27/14

I don't know if we had health insurance when I was a child. When I had an illness Mom's home remedies couldn't cure, I went to the doctor, and the rest of the time, I didn't give any thought to healthcare. Now our entire way of life revolves around the subject.

David's mother Betty is normally quite capable of taking care of herself in spite of health issues that require a care routine that would confound a trained professional. However, she recently fell, breaking her arm and tearing tendons in her foot making in necessary for her to have help. She was staying with her daughter Deb, but when Deb had to go out of town last week, David and I offered to fill in for her. While we were there, I was reminded what a hold health insurance has on our lives.

Being a patient has never been fun, but as the face of healthcare changes, it becomes even less so. When I had those childhood bouts of tonsillitis, no appointment was necessary to see the doctor, and time spent in the waiting room was usually minimal. Now doctors spend so much time doing preventative medicine, doing check-ups and running tests that you can't get in to see them when you're actually sick. Betty has a dozen cards on the front of her refrigerator, reminding of her of appointments, some of which are almost a year away.

In simpler times, doctors made decisions based on their education and experience. Now insurance companies take an active part in care plans. Unfortunately, in many cases, the resulting changes cost more, both to the consumer and to the insurance company. During my stint as a caregiver, I ran into the twenty-one-day rehab rule with Mom and Dad. In both cases, the patient had to stay in rehab longer than medically necessary in order for Medicare to cover the costs.

Medications are not exempt from this kind of micromanagement. In the short time we were with Betty, we dealt more than once with the complications of her Part D medication coverage.

Government participation in healthcare is also causing other negative effects. When I cared for Mom and Dad, one of their doctors closed his practice because of the unmanageable cost of a government-mandated computer system. In addition, my primary care physician here in Texas went on the system shortly after I started seeing him. His long-time nurse who was one of the stars of his practice retired rather than deal with it. Appointments take much longer as both nurses and doctors make notes on laptops rather than in paper files, and some doctors have cut their case loads as a result.

The national healthcare computer system and the "big brother" database it has developed can be more than a little disconcerting. When presenting a prescription at a pharmacy, even if you have never done business there, the computer pulls ups all your personal information with little or no help from you. I'm not generally a suspicious or paranoid person, but in this day of rampant identity theft, it's more than a little scary.

Healthcare used to be the last thing on my mind. Now it seems to be in the forefront of not only health concerns but also financial, political, and privacy concerns. Maybe it's a sign of the age in which we live, or maybe it's just a sign of my own "attained" age. Either way, it has become a bigger pain than the occasional sore throat.

CHAPTER 98

For Mattias: How TV Was Different when I Was a Kid – 8/31/14

We just got back from week with our kids and grandkids. Christian and Amy are wonderful people, great hosts, and interesting company, but Mattias and Zoe were the main attractions.

Zoe is four years old and is little Miss Sunshine personified. She is always smiling and rarely argues, and she fell in love with Grandpa David. I got my share of love from her, though, and we had fun planting seeds and going to the park.

Mattias is a more serious nine-year-old. He gives see-you-after-school waves and good-night hugs, but most of his interaction is verbal. He likes to talk and ask questions. One of his favorite questions is *How were things different when you were a kid?* I answered some of his questions, but I'm sure there are lots of differences left to explore. I've decided to devote a little space to the distant pass from time to time, so Mattias, this post is for you.

I was six years old the first time I saw a TV. We lived in west Texas in a small town near Abilene called Snyder. Our neighbors invited us over one Sunday night to see their new television set. It was very different from the wide, flat screens of today. It looked like a big, bulging eye in a square wooden box, and the picture was more sepia than black and white. Even with the outside antenna that looked like it was a mile high, Ed Sullivan was a little blurry and distorted on the round picture tube.

That summer we moved to Mesquite, a suburb of Dallas, and a couple of years later we got a TV of our own. Our house was small with only one living area, and Mom didn't want us sitting on the "good" furniture, so the TV was in the corner of the combination kitchen/dining room. We had a plastic and chrome dinette set, and we pulled the chairs around in front of the set when our "shows" came on. My favorite place to sit, however, was on the floor under the table. From there it was easy to scoot out and change the channel or adjust the volume. There was no remote control.

TV repair was a do-it-yourself affair. The back of the set was filled with vacuum tubes that looked a little like small fluorescent light bulbs. When the TV set went on the blink, Dad looked for any tubes that were discolored and took them to the testing machine at the supermarket. He plugged the suspicious tube into the proper spot, and if the meter showed a negative reading, he searched through the boxes of tubes on the shelf for a replacement. This usually worked, but sometimes it took a few trips to find the right bulb. If the huge picture tube went out, it was time to shoot the set and put everyone out of their misery.

It was several more years before we got color, and we saw more of my brother's back than the TV. He considered it his personal responsibility to give us the best color possible, and he spent what seemed like hours fiddling with the mysterious knobs in the little hidden panel on the front of the set. The biggest challenges, though, was how we managed to find something to watch with only three channels.

CHAPTER 99

How TV Programming Was Different when I Was a Kid – 9/7/14

Last week I wrote about how TVs were different in the olden days, but TV programming was a lot different, too. For one thing, there wasn't nearly as much to choose from. When we got our first set, we only had three channels. For another thing, programming wasn't available twenty-four hours a day. The first news programs came on around 6:00 a.m., and the broadcast day ended at midnight with the playing of the National Anthem as Old Glory fluttered in the breeze. After a few minutes, the flag was replaced by a test pattern and a steady tone. After a suitable period, which I never stayed up to time, the test pattern was replaced by snow and static.

The programs themselves were different, too. There were no ratings, but if there had been, everything would have been rated G. There were no four-letter words or foul language of any kind, and the comedy was upbeat and slapstick rather than dark or suggestive. The most violent shows we watched were *Mighty Mouse* and the *Road Runner* where poor Wiley Coyote was always being squashed by a piano or an Acme safe. There were lots of westerns, but even the most raucous fist fights never left split lips or black eyes. When someone got shot, he clutched his chest and fell melodramatically to the ground, but there was no blood. The only couples who lived together were married, and even they had twin beds. All the children said *Yes Ma'am* and *No Sir-* even Eddie Haskell, the *Leave It to Beaver* bad boy who was rather devious when the adults were not around.

Children's programming was limited to certain times of the day. *Romper Room* and *Captain Kangaroo* came on in the morning, and *Howdy Doody* and *Mickey Mouse Club* came on after school. *American Bandstand* with Dick Clark came later. It was cool, but no one danced too close together, and the boys usually wore coats and ties. Saturday morning was devoted to cartoons and the lighter westerns like *Roy Rogers* and the *Lone Ranger*. Instead of ads for action figures and other program-related paraphernalia, the commercials were for things like Tang, Nestles "Very Best" Chaaaawclate, and Ipana toothpaste.

I'm sure there were sports programs then, but I don't remember much except an occasional Harlem Globetrotter basketball game - and wrestling. We were wrestling fans, and it was very different in those days. The wrestlers wore regular wrestling gear and were mostly clean-cut, although there were a few bad boys on the circuit. Our favorite wrestler was Pepper Gomez - he was one of the good guys. Then Duke Keomuka came along with his "claw" hold, and things began to change. Instead of standard wrestling moves, they started doing strange things like standing on the corner posts and jumping on their opponents, and they started wearing costumes and trash talking before the matches. We gradually lost interest in wrestling and switched to other programs like *Your Hit Parade* and *Bonanza*.

Your Hit Parade was Mom's favorite, except for *Lawrence Welk*, of course. It was the 50s version of MTV, with a countdown of the top ten songs of the week performed live by Gisele MacKenzie, Snooky Lanson, and friends. It aired on Saturday night and was good, clean fun. *Bonanza*, on the other hand, was the end of society as we knew it according to many sermons on misplaced priorities. *Bonanza* aired on Sunday night, and along with *Wonderful World of Disney*, it enticed the faithful to sit in front of the TV instead of in the pews.

I could go on, but you get the idea. The next time you can't find anything interesting to watch on 120 channels, pull up an old *I Love Lucy* episode or a *Mighty Mouse* cartoon on Hulu. If you're a Baby Boomer like me, it will bring back fond memories. If you're younger, you might be surprised just how entertaining some of the oldies can be.

CHAPTER 100

We Dressed Differently when I Was a Kid – 9/14/14

Last year when we visited our kids and grandkids in Portland, I spent a good deal of time talking with Mattias, the nine year old. He likes to talk - a lot - and he asks lots of questions. One of his favorites is *How were things different when you were a kid?* The last couple of weeks, I wrote about how TV and TV programming were different. This is the next in the series.

We dressed a lot differently in the 50s and 60s than kids do now. One of the big differences was shoes. Shoes were usually made of leather, had smooth soles, and were brown or black. Tennis shoes were for gym class and the tennis court, and there were two choices - black high tops for the boys and white Keds for the girls.

The most popular shoe for school was penny loafers that had an open slot across the instep for a shiny, new penny. Some of the flashier kids put dimes in their shoes, but those of us who knew the value of a penny covered our pennies with foil and saved our dimes for more important things like candy and ice cream. Boys wore lace-up dress shoes to church, and girls wore flats or Mary Janes with straps. Play shoes were those that had become too scuffed and worn to be acceptable for school or church.

Girls wore bobby sox with our loafers, thick white sox that came halfway up our calves until we turned them down two or three turns to form a thick band around our ankles. Later, we evolved to crew sox. We wore thinner sox with our Sunday shoes, sometimes with a touch of lace around the edge. Boys wore white crew sox, some with a band of color around the top. Sometimes they switched to dark sox for Sunday, but sometimes they didn't.

Boys dressed a lot like they do today - shirts and pants - but there were some differences, especially on Sundays. Some actually wore suits, and the ones who didn't usually wore dress shirts with ties. For school they wore slacks or khakis or jeans. There were no designer jeans - the choices were Levis or Lees - and they were worn belted at the waist. The bottoms didn't puddle around the shoe tops or drag on the ground but instead were rolled up to expose an inch or two of white sock.

The biggest difference for boys was in the shirts. They all had collars and buttons. T-shirts were white undergarments that were not worn on the outside unless you were in the cast of *West Side Story* or were a wannabe hoodlum with one cigarette behind your ear and a pack rolled up in the sleeve of your t-shirt.

Girls wore dresses or skirts and blouses - period. Oh, we wore slacks or jeans to school on pep rally days, but otherwise they were forbidden. And we never, ever wore them to church.

There was a distinct difference in the way girls and women dressed. The emphasis for girls was sweet and wholesome, and anything revealing or sexy immediately labeled you as one of "those" girls. Hose and heels were reserved for those who had reached their teens, and the circular, gathered, and pleated skirts we wore were below the knee. The first time Mom made a "straight" skirt for me, she hemmed it at the middle of my knee. When I modeled it for Dad, he scowled.

"Looks awfully short to me," he said.

Hems became quite a point of contention between students and staff by the time I reached high school. To test the suitability of a skirt, the wearer had to kneel on the floor. If the hem didn't touch the tile, she was sent home to change.

Shorts were not much of an issue because we didn't wear them except in gym class or for playing outside in the heat of summer. Even then, most of us wore Bermudas just above the knee. Some of the more daring girls wore Jamaicas at mid-thigh, but again, only "those" girls wore short shorts.

If you're too young to remember any of this, get your grandparents to show you their high school yearbooks, or tune in an old episode of *Happy Days* and you'll get the idea.

CHAPTER 101

The Value of a Penny Was a Lot Different When I Was a Kid – 9/28/14

Most people don't get too excited about a penny any more. They walk away without waiting for the few cents change they have coming, and many don't bother to stoop over and pick up a penny. However, when I was a kid, a penny really meant something.

You could buy a bottled soft drink for five pennies. There were no machines to dispense ice-cold cans at the push of a button. Instead the 6.5 oz. glass bottles were chilled in a metal chest where they were suspended by the neck in rows between metal bars. You dropped your nickel in the slot, made your selection, slid the bottle to the end of the row, and lifted it out through a hinged metal flap. Dad was very frugal, and soft drinks were a rare treat. When the price went up to six cents, they became even rarer. In 1955, Coca-Cola introduced ten and twelve-oz. king-sized bottles that cost a dime, and our consumption dropped to almost zero for a while.

We moved to Mesquite, Texas, the summer between my first and second grade years. One of the main reasons was to get away from the dry, dusty climate that irritated my brother's bronchitis. Another reason was that Mom and Dad's brother and sister, who incidentally were married to each other, lived there. We visited their house more often than they visited ours because they had lots more kids and lots more space for us to run around without disturbing the neighbors. They also lived within walking distance of Pate's, an independent forerunner of the modern-day convenience store. Sometimes after a lunch of bologna sandwiches, each kid was given a nickel to spend on anything we wanted.

Pate's had a wide selection of ice cream bars, but those cost a whole nickel and had to be eaten quickly in the Texas heat. More often we opted for penny candy and spent what seemed like hours pooling our assets to maximize our buying power. *If I buy two Kits for a penny and you buy two Bit-O-Honeys for a penny, we can swap and still have eight cents left.*

Mesquite had one movie theater called the Ritz. It didn't live up to its name, but we thought it was wonderful. For less than fifty cents you could spend the afternoon in air conditioned comfort watching the movie as many times as you wanted and munching on enough snacks to ruin your dinner. If memory serves, there was only one size of popcorn, but other snack items followed Coca-Cola's lead in offering king-sized versions. Regular candy bars were larger than they are today, and they only cost a nickel. For a dime, you could buy a bar big enough to last until the cartoon rolled around again.

Ice cream cones were similar. This was before thirty-one flavors and marble slab creameries, but the Dairy Mart offered a delicious soft-serve ice cream. The nickel cone was comparable to a two-scooper, but if you super-sized to the dime cone, you had to make a choice between eating it so fast you got brain freeze or licking it off your hand as it melted down the side of the cone.

Sounds awesome, right? But keep in mind that incomes were proportionately small. My first allowance was fifty cents a week, and it rose through the years to a high of $1.50. Instead of the almost $5 average tooth fairy visit of today, lost teeth were worth about the price of a king-sized cone or candy bar.

I was amazed last year when I watch the commercial where a woman paid her babysitter forty dollars for the evening and then tipped her another twenty dollars for helping her daughter with a school project. The most I ever got for babysitting was fifty cents an hour. One family had four boys, and I tried to charge more, but I guess my bargaining skills weren't up to it. On my 16th birthday I applied for a job at Woolworth's at the Big Town Mall and was hired on at ninety cents an hour - a far cry from the fifteen dollars Walmart and McDonald's workers are asking today.

No, a penny isn't very exciting these days, but I still stoop over and pick one up if I see it lying on the ground. If I pick up enough of them, I might be able to buy an ice cream cone, and besides, it's good exercise.

CHAPTER 102

Cars Were a Lot Different When I Was a Kid – 10/5/14

All cars looked pretty much alike when I was a kid, at least to me, and they were all a lot different than cars today. Those who know about the inner workings of cars would probably say the engines are the biggest difference. In the olden days, everything under the hood was mechanical instead of computerized, but since I don't know a piston from a spark plug, I'll skip that discussion and move on to things I understand.

A lot of things that are taken for granted now were either not available or came as options. I don't think we had a radio in the car until I was older, and I know we didn't have air conditioning. If we drove any distance during the hot weather, we either went at night or bought a block of ice and put it in a dishpan on the floor in front of the vent in the hopes of cooling things off a bit.

Outside rear view mirrors were optional, too. One of the Christmas gifts Dad was most excited about was outside rear view mirrors.

He was doubly excited that there was one for each side and not just one for the driver's side.

There were no bucket seats, only bench seats that went from one door to another, and the gear shift was on the steering column instead of on a floor console. The seating arrangements might not have been as safe as they are today, but a girl could sit close to her fellow, and many a young woman learned to shift gears while her beau had his shifting arm draped around her shoulders. There were no other controls on the steering column. The driver indicated his intentions by sticking his left arm out the window in the manner prescribed by the state instead of by flashing amber turn signals or red brake lights. The intensity of the headlights was controlled by a foot-operated button on the floor to the left of the brake pedal, and the wipers were controlled by a button on the dashboard.

There were no car alarms or fancy electronic controls. Trunks were locked and unlocked with keys, and doors locks were controlled with keys or buttons that pushed down and pulled up. There were small triangular vent windows in the front doors that operated on a pivot system, and the bigger windows rolled up and down with a crank.

There were no safety features like child safety locks, child seats, or seat belts. I sometimes stood on the seat by Dad, tucked behind his right shoulder while he drove. I also remember sitting in his lap and "driving" the car. There was no safety glass either. On one outing I was kneeling backward in the front seat, looking out the rear window, when a rock hit the windshield, scattering bits of glass all over the backs of my legs.

I'm sure there are a lot more differences, like the amount of chrome and the price, but these are the differences I remember the most. How about you? What do you remember about cars from your earlier years?

CHAPTER 103

Grandparents Were a Lot Different when I Was a Kid – 10/12/14

My grandparent situation was a lot different when I was a kid than it is today. For one thing, I only had three grandparents instead the multitude of grandparents in some blended families. My dad's parents were still married to their original spouses, and my mom's mother was a widow. Her husband died several years before I was born.

My grandparents had strange names. Mom's father was Ralph Charles Hagan which wasn't too unusual, but her mother was Alva Lee (Cox) Hagan. Dad's father was Oscar Lee Robinson and his mother was Iona Florence (Yandall) Robinson. Not quite the same as David, Linda, and other contemporary names. It didn't matter that much because we didn't call them by their first names anyway.

My grandparents were also a lot older than many modern grandparents. My dad had three older sisters and three older brothers, and his oldest sister was twenty years older than he was.

Older people dressed different then. Grandmother Robinson had hair down to her waist, and she wore it up in a bun. Both grandmothers wore "sensible" shoes, black lace-ups or "Mary Janes" with wide one-inch heels. Granny Hagan dressed in a fairly stylish way, but Grandmother Robinson wore simple shirtwaist dresses. I never saw either of them in pants.

We saw the Robinson grandparents at family reunions every year, and we occasionally visited them at their small home in Abilene. When we arrived, Jim and I went in to say hello and give hugs, and then we went outside to play while the grownups visited. If it rained and we had to stay inside, there wasn't much to do. There was no TV and no toys. Grandmother did have a collection of empty wooden spools that had once held thread. We used them as bubble pipes by wetting one end, rubbing it across a bar of soap, and blowing through the hole in the other end. The spools also made good building blocks for kids with an active imagination.

The only other "toy" was Granddaddy's magnifying glass. He got it when his sight began to fade as his diabetes got worse, but after he lost his sight altogether, it took its place on the shelf beside the spools. We weren't allowed to take it outside where we could fry ants with it, but we had fun looking at the big version of everything in the house.

Granny Hagan lived in Dallas, so we saw her more often. She worked as a live-in housekeeper and caregiver for a woman and her invalid mother. The first place I remember visiting her was in a big, old house in Highland Park. Her living quarters were in a large room off the kitchen, and she had a fascinating Murphy bed on one wall. Her employer liked jigsaw puzzles, and when she finished one, she passed it on to Granny. Her work in progress was always spread out on a card table in the corner, and I loved to try and find a piece or two when I visited.

Then they moved to a more modern house, and Granny had her own apartment with a standard bed. It wasn't nearly as interesting, but we never stayed very long. We usually picked her up on her day off and took her home to spend the afternoon with us. Once we were home, she visited with Mom and Dad while we went about our usual business as kids, but I always wanted to sit by her in the car on the way home.

Even though she didn't play with us, she took a more active role in our lives than the Robinson grandparents. She didn't have much money for gifts, but she was an excellent seamstress. She bought fabric remnants and made custom outfits for the granddaughters' dolls or smocked throw pillows for our beds. I'm not sure what she did for the boys. When we went away to college, she wrote letters each week and enclosed a dollar.

My grandparents never took me to Disneyland or showered me with gifts, but I have fond memories of good cooking and warm hugs. They were simple people with simple lives, and those lives included a simple love for their grandchildren.

CHAPTER 104

A Walk Down Memory Lane – 21st Century Style – 6/7/15

David and I had an unexpected and really fun date night last week. It was unexpected first, because it happened Saturday morning, and second, because we thought we were going to meet some of our Senior Center friends at a local church for their monthly breakfast. There had been a change of schedule, though, and we didn't get the memo. When we arrived, the parking lot was empty and the doors were closed and locked.

As David turned the car around and headed back toward Emory, I wondered what I had in the refrigerator at home. I didn't have to wonder long, though.

"Do you want to stop at Sidekick's and have some breakfast?" David asked.

I did. We found a table close to the back so David could see the TV, but he didn't look at it much. He told me about a post on Facebook that asked what from the 1950s would be the hardest to explain to someone from the 21st century. The suggested answer was a book, something without batteries you could hold in your hand and find any information you might need. We laughed and decided it might be even harder to explain a physical card catalog and a library that offered more printed material than e-books, audio books, DVDs, and computers.

Then, I noticed David looking over my shoulder. I thought he was looking at the TV, but he was checking out the picture on the wall behind me that featured all the western personas of Clint Eastwood. We spent a few minutes looking around at all the cowboys on the wall until David said, "I thought this was supposed to be Sidekick's. Where are the pictures of Tonto and Cisco?"

Our food had arrived by this time, but we continued our discussion of cowboy buddies while we ate. Our memories failed us in some cases, but we used the 21st century research method by consulting my cell phone from time to time. We remembered that Roy Rogers had two different sidekicks - besides Dale Evans, of course. Their TV names were Pat Brady and Cookie. We had to use Google to find that the name of Zorro's friend was Bernardo.

The conversation eventually veered off into the many western series that were on TV when we were growing up. There were as many of those as there are cop shows now. We continued to talk through a couple of extra cups of coffee and then headed home to work in the yard.

Pulling weeds when the temperature is bumping up against ninety degrees isn't a lot of fun, but thinking back on our walk down memory lane made the time pass quickly. I think we'll have to take the time to be spontaneous more often.

CHAPTER 105

How did we survive? – 7/19/15

"It's 99 outside, feels like 101," said David, looking at the weather on his phone. "Triple digits for at least the next week. I don't know how we survived before air conditioning."

We've had this same conversation several times since summer finally came to Texas - especially when our air conditioning unit stopped working the Thursday before the Fourth of July. For several days David worked with a repairman and two helpful neighbors, but due to a series of replacement parts that were unavailable or didn't work, our central unit sat idle until Monday. Thankfully, we had installed a window unit in the bedroom a few weeks before, so we survived the weekend by closing ourselves in and watching lots of old movies - and we talked about how we kept cool before Freon became available to the masses.

One of the favorite ways to beat the heat when I was a kid was water. Keep in mind that I am one generation removed from West Texas tenant farmers, so no one I knew owned a swimming pool. When Mom and Dad were young and swimsuit fit, we sometimes went on family outings to the public swimming pool, and when I was a little older, I occasionally went to the pool with my friends. More often, though, we stayed home, and the kids played with the hose. While supposedly watering the flowers, we turned the spray nozzle on each other, and when Dad watered the lawn, we had a great time running through the sprinklers. We didn't have a real wading pool, so we filled an old Number 2 Washtub and took turns jumping off the porch and making a splash.

Another way of escaping the heat was to follow the example of the wealthy who spent their summers in the mountains or at the seashore. We didn't travel in style, but we did get away from time to time. We visited relatives on the Gulf and played in the waves. It wasn't much cooler there than home, but it was fun. Sometimes we spent a week in the Ozarks where we experienced some real relief. Since our car wasn't air conditioned, the trip itself wasn't much fun, but we always left early enough to make it to our destination before the sun was too high in the sky. If the heat became too oppressive, Dad would stop and buy a bag of crushed ice. He set it in a dishpan on the floor in front of the vent to cool the air as it blew into the car. We also chewed on the ice to cool off our insides.

When we were at home and inside, we had fans - a small oscillating fan in each bedroom to move the hot air around a bit. As technology and finances advanced, we added an evaporative cooler in the master bedroom. During the hottest part of the day, I'd spread a quilt on the floor in front of the cooler and spend a couple of hours reading or napping. Later, we moved to a house that had an attic fan. It pulled air in through the windows so that, even though the night air wasn't very cool, at least it was fresh. Eventually, Mom and Dad bought a window unit for their bedroom, and not long afterward, they added another one in the den. The house was small enough that the two units kept it relatively comfortable.

My first experience with central air conditioning was when I moved into an apartment when I was twenty, and I haven't lived without it since. I have survived the Texas heat with nothing more than a water hose and a fan, and I could probably do it again. Hopefully, though, I won't have to.

POTPOURRI

CHAPTER 106

Feeling Old – 1/18/15

I'm feeling a little old lately. This afternoon I even dozed off for a few minutes during the football game. Not for long, though, because I woke up when I heard David snapping a picture of me, a photo that will probably end up on Facebook. There was a time when a person could grab a few winks on a Sunday afternoon without being harassed by the paparazzi, but at least I had my mouth closed - I think.

One reason I'm feeling a bit on the elderly side is strictly physical. Yesterday I worked in the garden for a few hours, and my body is a little mad at me today. I feel fine as long as I'm sitting still, but every time I sit or stand or otherwise shift positions, those muscles that I haven't used in a couple of months protest rather vigorously.

Aside from the physical, there are other reasons I'm feeling my age. For one thing, our granddaughter just had her sixth birthday. We couldn't go to Oregon to celebrate, but we had a Face Time conversation with her. She is so grown up that I had visions of her in a cap and gown and maybe even a wedding dress, and I sighed as I envisioned the years flying by.

As if that weren't enough, our son has been complaining about his advancing age. He's a young forty-three, but he was recently shocked when he was offered a senior discount at the grocery store. His fading youth was further insulted when his eye doctor prescribed bifocals. He tried to soften the blow by calling them transitional lenses, but the damage was done. He and I both felt the years piling up.

All of this was bad, but the thing that has made me feel the oldest is an email I received last week announcing plans for a high school class reunion - the fiftieth. Yes, it has been fifty years since I donned my own cap and gown and celebrated the successful completion of twelve years of education. My class is not very active, so our last reunion was thirty years ago. However, thanks to the Internet and social media, no one will expect us to be as young and beautiful as we were then. This time, instead of comparing careers and children, we'll probably be competing to see who has had the most joints replaced and whose grandchildren are superior. It will be fun to reminisce and reconnect, but the coming event adds to my feelings of advancing age.

It's not all bad, though. As for the physical aches and pains, a few pain pills and a hot shower or two will make me feel normal again. When it comes to my aging son and my growing grandchildren, I'm in reasonably good health, and with the Good Lord's help, I'll have the privilege of celebrating many important life events with them. The reunion? I still have mixed feelings, but I'll probably go, and I'll probably enjoy it. After all, my grandchildren are definitely the most beautiful and the most brilliant.

CHAPTER 107

It's the Small Things – 2/01/15

In 1996, Dr. Richard Carlson published a book called ***Don't Sweat the Small Stuff...and It's All Small Stuff***. The purpose of the book was to tell readers how to keep from letting the little things in life drive them crazy. We live in a microwave world where everything is done in a hurry, and stress is the rule rather than the exception. Even the most laid back, small-town retiree has only to turn on the nightly news to be pulled back into the pressure-cooker society he or she moved to the country to escape.

While there are plenty of big issues to cause anxiety, it's also true that the small irritations are sometimes what push us over the edge. The CEO of a Fortune 500 company may clinch a deal with a most difficult client without breaking a sweat only to blow up when a careless clerk orders the wrong color sticky notes. In the private sector, the most patient wife may become a raging shrew when the lid is left up once too often, while her long-suffering husband may lose his cool when she moves the remote control from his favorite spot.

On the other hand, sometimes it's the small things that bring us pleasure. I once had a friend who didn't like tomatoes. When he came for dinner, I made a point of putting his salad in a separate bowl before I added the offending ingredient. It amazed me how special he felt when I not only remembered his preference but also considered it when making the meal preparations.

Life offers us lots of opportunities to make life better for those around us in small ways. Campaigns promoting random acts of kindness have been popular in the last several years. Most of these acts are directed toward strangers, but small acts of consideration directed toward those we know and love can have a powerful effect. Hanging his shirts so they all face the same direction or fixing her coffee just the way she likes it will improve your marriage, and putting the toilet paper on the roller in the direction your spouse prefers may save the marriage altogether.

Last week I was on the receiving end of a small thing. It made my day, and I still smile every time I think about it. Several months ago, on the advice of my doctor, we cut wheat products out of our diet. Since most gluten-free breads are very expensive, we've been pretty much bread free. I recently complained on Facebook that one of the collateral results of not buying bread is a definite lack of twisties.

There was a time when food storage and trash bags came with twisties, and there were always more of the little wire closers than bags. These leftovers, plus the ones from bread, ensured that there were always plenty on hand for closing that open bag of rice or that partial bag of frozen veggies. Now, I'm down to a few remaining ties, and chip clips or rubber bands just don't work well in every situation.

Friday, we had hamburgers for lunch at the Senior Center. With most of the meals, we have rolls or cornbread that come in metal warming trays, but hamburgers come with buns - in bags - with twisties. I didn't give it any thought until I started to leave, and I heard Margaret call my name.

"Hey, Linda. I have something for you."

Wondering what it could be, I went to the kitchen where she handed me three twisties. We both laughed at the gift, but I felt kind of warm and fuzzy. She had not only remembered my complaint but had also taken a minute to do something about it. Sometimes it really is the small things.

CHAPTER 108

Nightwalk for Hope Rained Out – 5/10/15

Slavery was abolished in the United States in 1865, but did you know that, according to a story released by KLTV on August 24, 2013, that a form of slavery called human trafficking is a growing problem - not in Africa or Asia or New York, but in East Texas. Human trafficking is defined as *the illegal movement of people, typically for the purposes of forced labor or commercial sexual exploitation.* Traffickers often target at risk young people, sometimes twelve-years-olds and younger, in order to sell their bodies for cash. A Tyler expert was quoted by KLTV as saying that, in Smith County, 33% of girls and 17% of boys will be sexually abused, some of them at the hand of traffickers, before the age of eighteen.

For the Silent is a non-profit organization based in Tyler and dedicated to bringing *hope to teens silenced by sex trafficking and exploitation in the United States through prevention, intervention and community mobilization programs.* Their second annual Nightwalk for Hope was scheduled for April 24, but due to stormy weather, it was rescheduled for May 8. The event featured a two-mile walk through Rose Rudman Park with music and other activities planned at the finish line. During the walk, each participant would carry a lantern to symbolize hope and freedom for those silenced by human trafficking.

Friday night, ten members of Believers' Baptist Church, along with many others, congregated at the park. We were excited, both about the fellowship and also about helping to raise awareness and funds for a cause that touched us all deeply. We met at the pre-arranged spot near the sign-in tables where those who had pre-registered on-line and given the recommended donation of $10 each picked up their t-shirts. David and I had not pre-registered, so I filled out the required forms while he pulled out his wallet and looked around for the donation box.

Before he found the box, the sky was illuminated by a huge bolt of lightning followed by deafening clap of thunder, and the rain that had threatened all the way from Emory began to fall. Our small group scattered with the guys heading for the truck and the gals opting for the covered pavilion that was a short jog away. We avoided getting too wet, and our spirits weren't dampened. We used our phones to take pictures of each other and to check the progress of the huge green, yellow, and red blob that was fast approaching Tyler from the southwest.

The lightning continued to flash, and the rain fell harder. About thirty minutes before the sunset walk was scheduled to begin, we saw people walking toward their cars, and we heard several of them say that the walk had been canceled. One couple braved the rain to check on the rumor, and when they returned with confirmation, our small band said goodnight and split up. David and I had carpooled with another couple, so she and I waited under the pavilion while the guys navigated the traffic to get as close to us as possible. Once we were in the truck, we made one more stop so David could make a mad dash back to the donation box to drop in the money that had been crumpled in his pocket all evening. Then, we headed back to Emory.

On the way, we stopped in Lindale for ice cream and chit chat. When we returned to the vehicle to make our way home, we laughed at our mature version of a Texas double date - a pick-up truck at the Dairy Queen with guys in front seat and gals in back. It was funny, but I couldn't help but wonder about those kids in Tyler and other small towns across America who find nothing to laugh about in a world where there seems to be nothing but despair.

Still, there will be another Nightwalk next year, and as long as there are organizations like For the Silent, there is still hope. If you would like to learn more about For the Silent and how you can donate or get involved, go to www.ForTheSilent.org or call 903-747-8128.

CHAPTER 109

Mass Shooters: Are they shouting, "Look at me?" – 6/30/15

On June 17, a twenty-one-year-old man shot and killed nine people during a Bible study at the Emanuel African Methodist Episcopal Church in Charleston, South Carolina. His website consists of white supremacist diatribes and apparently features a picture in which he is posing with a handgun in front of a Confederate flag. It has been reported that he shouted racial slurs during the attack and that he later told police that his purpose was to start a race war. One account said he almost didn't go through with the attack because the victims were so nice to him. I couldn't help but wonder what circumstances in his twenty-one years might have prevented the attack altogether.

If you've raised children of your own or been around children for any length of time, you're probably familiar with the look-at-me phenomenon. After "no" and "mine," I think the next words a child learns are "look at me." The plea is repeated at a steadily increasing volume until the desired attention is achieved, and then some amazing feat is performed - a six-inch jump, a lop-sided cartwheel, a swoop down the slide, or a splashing belly flop into the kiddie pool. Whatever the act, it is always followed by a tentative grin as the actor waits hopefully for the sought after affirmation that he or she is special and important to you.

In the olden days of stay-at-home moms and dinner around the dining room table every night, one-on-one recognition and acknowledgment of a person's individuality seemed fairly easy to come by. However, as family structure has changed and screens of all sorts shout for attention, a child may find it harder to find the attention he seeks. Instead of competing with a few siblings, she may be one of ten or twenty children wanting to be noticed by a teacher or child care worker.

This decreasing individual attention along with increased access to media has created a desire for a larger audience. When recent polls asked what teens wanted to be when they grew up, the most common answer was "famous," and both reality TV and the Internet have made fame a possibility. If a person doesn't have a prize-winning talent, he can become a star by having the most "likes" of a recent selfie, the most blog views, or the highest body count in the latest video game. It sounds like harmless fun until, tragically, someone in Columbine, Sandy Hook, or Emanuel AME Church takes it to the ultimate level.

Since June 17, there has been a flood of anger, sorrow, and disbelief at the senseless loss of life. There has also been a flurry of activity seeking to remove anything that might have caused, fed, or facilitated the obsession that ended with yet another heartbreaking attack. A Confederate flag was removed from the grounds of the South Carolina Statehouse, and the sale of Confederate flags was discontinued by several major retailers. Interest was renewed in a petition to remove the Confederate carvings on Stone Mountain, Georgia, and a June 24 article in the New York Post by Lou

Lumenick suggested that maybe the movie *Gone with the Wind*, along with the Confederate flag, should *be consigned to museums as an ugly symbol of racism.*

It is normal, in the wake of a tragedy like this, to try to explain it, to find causes, to find a way to ensure that nothing like this ever happens again. This is an essential part of the healing process. However, it is important that we not center our attention on an emotionally charged meme that we can share on Facebook in order to feel like we have been part of the solution. It is also important that we focus, not only on the symptoms but also on the cause. There is no easy answer to why a person decides to become famous by ending the lives of innocent people, but I can't help but wonder if somewhere way back when, he wasn't simply a little boy saying, "Hey, look at me."

We can't go back in time and undo what has already been done, but there are children all around us who need attention now. You may have some in your own home who need, not just thirty minutes of quality time now and then, but who need constant reassurance that they matter. If you don't have children at home, there are countless opportunities to be involved in guiding lives into constructive paths. Churches are begging for volunteers to help with Sunday school, AWANA, Vacation Bible School, Camps, and other children's and youth activities. Schools and various organizations have students who go without mentors, tutors, big brothers and sisters, and more because too few people are available.

The movie "Avatar" features a race of beings called the Na'vi. When the Na'vi have deep feelings for one another, they don't say "I love you." Instead, they look deeply into one another's eyes and say, "I see you." I wonder how many tragedies could be averted if we really learned to see each other, especially our children.

CHAPTER 110

The Ladies of the Order of the Pink Ribbon – 11/8/15

Last week I talked about all the "national" months, weeks, and days that are on the American calendar. Specifically, I mentioned that November is National Family Caregiver Month and National Novel Writing Month. One very important month I didn't mention is October, which is Breast Cancer Awareness Month. Some of the months are pretty low key or have limited media appeal, but with all the special events and promotions, it's hard to miss this month, especially when 300 pound linebackers wear pink socks.

Even though the football players have gone back to their standard uniforms, the subject was on my mind last week, because it was time for me to go in for a mammogram. It's a very familiar procedure since I found my first cyst when I was sixteen, but so far, all of my test results have been good. Thursday morning, while I was getting ready to go to the lab, I thought about all the women who have not been as blessed as I have been, women who gone in for a diagnosis and have heard the word cancer.

Many of these women have been a part of my life, but in the last few years, there are several special ones that I have encountered on a close enough basis to be aware of some of the details of their struggles. I have been amazed by the humor, strength, and courage with which they have faced this formidable enemy. Some have won and have been pronounced cancer free, some are still in treatment, and some are facing the end of a losing battle – but regardless of the outcome of their fight, all of these women are heroes.

About ten years ago, David's Aunt Jerry had a mastectomy followed by a second one a couple of years later. She opted for prostheses rather than reconstructive surgery. She says the silicone forms are hot and uncomfortable, so when she's at home, she usually leaves them in the drawer. However, when it's time to go somewhere, her humor always showed up. "Give me a minute. I have to go put on the girls."

Several years later, when we first moved to Emory, we began going to Believers' Baptist Church. I was not aware that Tiny, the worship leader, was undergoing her own battle until she was added to the prayer list. She missed several services, and when she returned, she was sporting a stylish wig that was almost a perfect match for her natural hair. I complimented her new do, but she smiled and said, "I hate it! It's heavy, hot, and scratchy." It wasn't long before the wig gave way to a colorful scarf, but the turban was still too hot. Her desire to use her God-given gift was stronger than any vanity or concern with what people would think, and until the chemo was over and her hair grew back, she praised the Lord with a bare head.

A couple of years ago, a Florida friend named Cindy was told that her cancer had recurred. Since then, she has gone through several courses of treatment, but last month she was told that none of them had been effective, and she was moved into an in-house hospice facility. Her many friends have rallied around her, and one of them has taken on the task of helping her long-distance friends share this season of her life by posting updates and photographs. I have been amazed by the courage and faith Cindy has shown and the radiant smile she wears in every picture. Shortly after she moved into the facility, her friends gathered to share treasured memories and to show their love for her. As part of the decorations, a beautiful wedding dress was displayed in a corner, and Cindy wore a wedding veil. The caption on the party pictures read "Like a bride...Waiting for her groom...She'll be a church ready for you...Every heart longing for our King" I guess that explains the radiance – every bride is beautiful.

I'm dedicating this column to these heroic women and millions of others who have fought a good fight. Whether they won or lost, each step adds to what we know about this dreadful disease. One of the things we know is that early detection is the key to survival. In honor of all those who have gone before, don't neglect your check-ups.

CHAPTER 111

Getting off the Interstate – 11/15/15

David and I spent almost the entire month of October on the road. We left home on October 2 and returned over six thousand miles later on October 29. The main destination as far as I was concerned was Beaverton, Oregon, a suburb of Portland where my two amazing grandchildren live. Their parents live there, too, but the grands were the main attraction.

When we were planning the trip, we decided to drive and do some visiting and sight-seeing along the way. We thought about taking the motor home, but since it needs some work, we opted for the car. My intention was to chronicle our adventures along the way, but the editors at the Leader pointed out that it's not wise to advertise the fact that one's home is vacant. With that in mind, and since I was too busy having fun to spend much time writing, I shared caregiving humor instead.

However, when I sat down to write this week's column, I flipped through the steno pad where I jot down grocery lists, to do lists, and an occasional inspiration. I came across a note I had scribbled early in the trip. It said: *You miss a lot of the good stuff when you stay on the Interstate.* Taking the narrow road and choosing the road less traveled are not new ideas, but sometimes life hands you an example that is too good not to share.

When we left Emory, we made a stop in Denver to visit a cousin I hadn't seen in ten years. Then, we headed into Wyoming to see the Tetons, Beartooth, and Yellowstone. After two days of marveling at the wonders of creation, we continued west. We usually stopped for the night at five o'clock, give or take an hour, so I checked the map and guessed that we'd be near Twin Falls, Idaho around that time. I used my phone to check for motels in the area, and let's just say that the motel owners in Twin Falls are very proud of their rooms, so I expanded my search area. I found a room at the Oregon Trail Inn in Buhl, Idaho, about twenty miles south and west of the Interstate. It looked like it would work, so I booked a room, entered the address into the GPS, and crossed my fingers.

The motel was small but well maintained; the room was large, comfortable, and very clean; and the staff was friendly and helpful. The best part of the experience came the next morning, though. We checked the map to see if there was a way to get back on the Interstate other than back-tracking the way we had come. State Highway 30 ran northwest out of Buhl and intersected with Interstate 84 in Bliss, Idaho. When David returned our key cards to the office, the motel manager assured us that, although Hwy 30 was mostly two lane, it was a nice, scenic drive, so we chose the narrower road.

The first few miles of the thirty mile trek took us through a very picturesque farming area. We could smell the onions as large tractor-like vehicles moved through the fields. I am, after all, a city girl, but it looked to me as if the onions were being topped in preparation for harvest. After about ten miles, the landscape began to change. We could see the Snake River on the east side of the road, and sheer rock cliffs rose vertically out of the flat land beyond the river. In several places, waterfalls gushed out of the flat rock faces. True to its name, the river wound around until it was on the west side of the road, and the land began to fall away. The road was eventually at a high enough elevation that we couldn't see what was below, so we pulled over to a scenic overlook to check it out. Stretched out in either direction was a river valley filled with farms green and idyllic enough to inspire poems, songs, and endless other artistic expressions.

A few minutes after our stop, we merged into the Interstate, and the scenery became flat and boring, with no hint of the beauty that lay just a few miles away. We were grateful for the circumstances that took us out of our way and into what turned out to be one of the highlights of our trip. Since we were not on a rigid schedule, we had several other opportunities to explore and several more chances to remember that life is a journey and not a destination.

CHAPTER 112

New Year's Day - What's It All About? – 12/27/14

David recently posed an interesting question. "I wonder why we celebrate New Year's Day."

In this era of the Internet and cell phones, I gave him my standard answer. "I don't know. Why don't you Google it."

He did, and he discovered that Julius Caesar, along with scientists of his day, completely revised the calendar, adding days, renaming the seventh month after himself, and shifting the beginning of the year from March to January. This Julian calendar, with a few minor tweaks, is still used by much of the world, but not all.

Later, I did a little research of my own, and I turned up a great deal of information. I knew the Chinese and the Jews follow a calendar of their own and that the Christian church has a liturgical calendar that differs from the Julian calendar, but I had no idea that there is a long list of civilizations that follow their own calendar.

This wealth of knowledge was interesting, but I was more interested in why we celebrate the beginning of a new year, regardless of when it is. Most of the information I found as to the "why" of the holiday was in blogs and articles in which the writers offered opinions. I decided that if I was going to rely on an opinion, I might as well use my own. My opinion is that it's all about fresh starts – not an original idea, but truth rarely is.

January 1 has become a day of new beginnings: beginning a diet that will get you into that special pair of jeans, starting an exercise program that will give you six-pack abs, setting up a budget that will get your finances in order, earning a degree that will qualify you for your dream job, writing that award-winning novel. In the immortal words of Dr. Phil, "How's that working out for you?"

As I've already demonstrated, in-depth research is not my strong suit, but the few articles I scanned agreed that many, if not most, New Year's resolutions don't last into February. The fresh fruits and vegetables soften and shrivel in the refrigerator while the fast food wrappers collect in the back seat of the car. The gym that was packed in early January is virtually deserted by Valentine's Day, and the shiny, new BowFlex has become a very expensive clothes rack. Credit card companies receive requests to replace "lost" cards that were cut into pieces in the enthusiasm of the New Year. The exhilaration of celebration has faded, and a sense of failure has taken its place.

In a much earlier season of my life, I spent a few years as an insurance agent. Anyone who has been involved in sales has probably received at least some training in goal setting. One technique is called the SMART method – make goals specific, measurable, attainable, relevant, and time-bound. It is also important to make both long-term and short-term goals and to review goals often, revising them as necessary.

I believe we often fail to achieve our goals because we make the time element too long. By that, I mean that we set a five-year goal and plan to review it annually, or we set a one-year goal and plan to review it monthly. Then, on week two, we leave the salad we brought for lunch in the office refrigerator and go out with co-workers for a burger and fries. We label ourselves as a failure, and we give up.

I wonder if we would have more success if we followed the twelve-step program model and took our New Year's resolutions one day at a time. Each evening, review how the day went. If you did good, reward yourself – in keeping with your goals, of course. No hot fudge sundaes for those on a diet or $200 shoes for those on a budget. On the other hand, if you blew it, review both the day and your plan. Adjust your plan if necessary, adjust your attitude as needed, and resolve to do better tomorrow.

This one-day-at-a-time approach is not a new idea either. The writer of the Book of Lamentations had this to say about it in the sixth century B.C.:

The steadfast love of the Lord never ceases;his mercies never come to an end;they are new every morning; great is your faithfulness.

New Year's Day comes once a year, and each new year feels like a clean slate. Still, every time the sun comes up, a new day presents its own clean slate. As those slates are filled with small successes, next year's celebration might just be a really big one.

Happy New Year!

ABOUT THE AUTHOR

Linda Brendle, a multi-genre Christian author, first began to write during her years as a caregiver. After two memoirs about Alzheimer's caregiving – *A Long and Winding Road and Mom's Long Good-Bye* – she ventured into the world of fiction. She has published a three-novel romantic suspense series, *Tatia's Tattoo, Fallen Angel Salvage*, and *Salvaged*. She has also published a light-hearted journal titled *Kitty's Story* about the feral cat who took over that Brendle household several years ago. Retired from the business world, Linda now blogs and writes for the weekly newspaper in the tiny East Texas town where she and her husband David live and take care of the needs and demands of Kitty.

MORE BOOKS BY LINDA BRENDLE

Tatia's Tattoo: As a successful D.C. lawyer, Tatia's mission in life is to destroy the sex trafficking trade in small-town America. She knows where to find it. She's been there. Filled with tragedy, crime, redemption, and love, Tatia's Tattoo is a story that exposes the sordid underbelly of small towns and shines a light of hope on how the evil might be defeated.

Fallen Angel Salvage (Tatia's Story, Book #2): Tatia and Jesse have a perfect life in Chicago. Her testimony put Eric in prison in Texas twenty years ago. How could anything go wrong? An old black van. A missing child. Tatia and Jesse race through the city streets with a band of bikers while Johnny and Jade dig through the dark web and Detectives Nelson and Martin pound on doors. Will it be enough? Or will their daughter become another statistic?

SALVAGED: Tatia's Story - Book #3: SALVAGED is the story of a young woman's struggle to recover the life that was stolen and hidden from her for fourteen years. Who is she? Where did she come from? Is there a future after Michael?

Tatia's family is recovering from Joy's dramatic rescue when their quiet Sunday afternoon is interrupted by the doorbell. Madison collapses into Joy's arms, bruised and trembling with symptoms of withdrawal. Who is this mysterious young woman whose phone call saved Joy from kidnappers and traffickers? And why is a Chicago crime boss looking for her?

A Long and Winding Road: A Caregiver's Tale of Life, Love, and Chaos: This memoir is the story of the hilarity and chaos that happen when four people, two of whom have Alzheimer's, spend seven weeks traveling through sixteen states in a forty-foot motor home. It is also the story of the lives and experiences that led these four people to this particular place and time in their lives.

Mom's Long Goodbye: A Caregiver's Tale of Alzheimer's, Grief, and Comfort: After finishing Winding Road, many readers asked what happened next. Mom's Long Goodbye is the rest of the story. Mom's goodbye began with a red photo album and ended fifteen years later in a hospital bed in the Alzheimer's wing of Southridge Village. This is her story and mine.

Kitty's Story: From Feral Kitten to Reigning House Cat: A four-ounce ball of black and white fur walked out from under the porch of an unsuspecting couple who had no intention of having any pets, much less a house cat. Four years later, she has grown into a beautiful, thirteen-pound semi-longhair tuxedo cat who reigns supreme over the Brendle household.

NEXT ON THE PRINTING PRESS!

But God...: A fictionalized version of the early life of a friend who lived in Holland during World War II and kept the secret of the Jewish couple who lived in his attic for two years.

www.ingramcontent.com/pod-product-compliance
Lightning Source LLC
Chambersburg PA
CBHW071229070526
44583CB00017B/2102